ANGLE
—— *of* ——
VISION

ANGLE

—— *of* ——

VISION

Christians and the Middle East

CHARLES A. KIMBALL

FRIENDSHIP PRESS • NEW YORK

Editorial Offices:
475 Riverside Drive, New York, NY 10115

Distribution Offices:
P.O. Box 37844, Cincinnati, OH 45222-0844

Manufactured in the United States of America

Library of Congress Cataloging-in-Publication Data

Kimball, Charles.
  Angle of vision : Christians and the Middle East / Charles A. Kimball.
  128 p.   cm.
  Includes bibliographical references.
  ISBN 0-377-00240-2 : $7.95
  1. Middle East—Church history. 2. Middle East—Religion. 3. Middle East—Politics and government—1979- I. Title.
BR1070.K56   1991
275.6—dc20   91-42506
                                                                       CIP

Bible quotations are from the New Revised Standard Version, copyright © 1989 by the Division of Education and Ministry of the National Council of the Churches of Christ in the U.S.A. Used by permission.

For
Gabriel Habib, Dick Butler and Dale Bishop
three friends and mentors
whose ministries with the churches in the Middle East
are living examples of ecumenism.

Contents

The Middle East

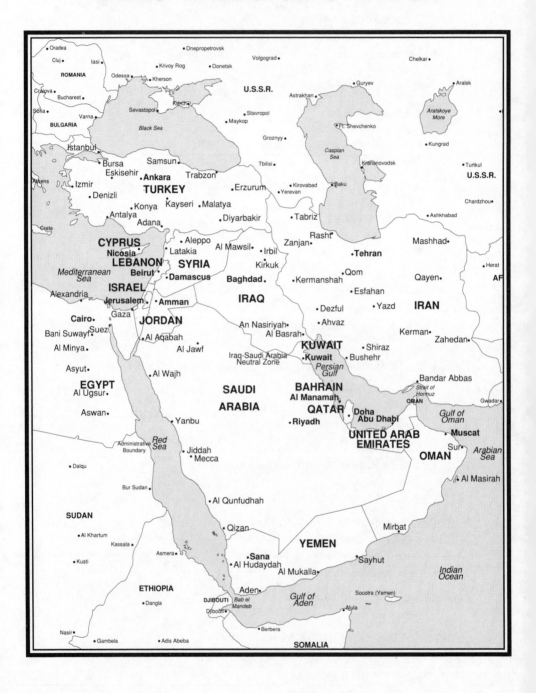

I

Our Common Heritage

OUR LINKS WITH THE MIDDLE EAST

A prominent Lebanese Christian leader tells about meeting with a young missionary couple several years ago. The missionaries had arrived recently from the U.S. and were expressing eagerness to begin their new ministry. "Under which missionary effort," one asked the Lebanese Christian, "did your family convert?" Without hesitation, he responded, "It was the missionary effort of the Apostle Paul!"

After a moment of stunned silence, the young American couple began to realize that the spread of the gospel in the Middle East did not begin with the modern Protestant missionary movement. Rather, the church began in these very lands. The first missionaries spread the "good news" from there throughout the world. The realization was startling and provocative for the young couple. Talking with someone whose Christian heritage is rooted in the soil of the earliest church provided a new perspective.

Like the missionary couple, most of us approach people and places outside our experience with many unconscious presuppositions. When we in the Western countries encounter the Middle East, we bring our own point of view. The very name commonly used for this part of the world illustrates the point. Why do we call it the "Middle East"? "East" of where? "Middle" in relation to what? This term and the older "Near East" reflect a Euro-centric orientation. If you assume that Europe is the "center" of world civilization, then the terms make sense. In relation to Europe, the region including China, Japan and Korea is the "Far East"; the lands roughly halfway to the Far East are the "Near East" or "Middle East." Yet this way of viewing and speaking about the world does not reflect reality from the perspective of the people in that region. They do not see themselves as "midway" to somewhere; they are simply in their native homeland.

The different ways people perceive the rest of the world are influenced by many cultural, religious and historical factors. Sharpening our awareness of these factors, including our own presuppositions and biases, helps us approach an area like the Middle East in a more honest and accurate way. This does not mean, however, that we must jettison generic terms like "the West" and "Middle East." They can serve as useful categories. When we speak of "Western Christian perspectives on Islam," for instance, we are using a convenient shorthand to refer to the attitudes of the majority Protestant and Roman Catholic communities in North America and Europe. By contrast, "Middle Eastern Christian views on Islam" refers to those of the predominantly Orthodox communities that have lived together with Muslims for fourteen centuries.

As Western Christians, we carry considerably more intellectual and emotional baggage than we realize. Our angle of vision has been shaped, and sometimes confused, by a variety of connections with this region of the world. Some of these connections are direct. For example, a nephew may have lived and worked in Saudi Arabia for several years. Some are woven into our religious heritage. Without question, most Christians feel some degree of affinity with names and places that provide the framework for biblical history: Jerusalem, Damascus, the Jordan River, Sinai, Egypt, and so forth. Some connections have been urged on us by the history we learned in school and by more recent news: we have been inundated with television images of conflict and violence through several decades of strife.

The swirl of biblical and historical images combined with perceptions of contemporary religious, political and cultural developments often creates confusion. Without an effort to clarify some of these connections, many people are perplexed over their feelings about events in this ancient and fascinating crossroads of civilization. Let us look more closely at some major ways North Americans are linked with the Middle East.

The Children of Abraham and the Holy Land

Jews, Christians and Muslims share an abiding attachment to the Middle East. The roots run deep and the sense of connection is strong because people in all three religious traditions worship God in the tradition of Abraham, their patriarch. The formative history of each community of faith, whether viewed independently or in relationship with the other two, is intimately connected with the areas we call the Holy Land today.

Jerusalem, the "city of peace," stands at the symbolic center, the converging point for the three great monotheistic communities. In an almost mystical way, Jerusalem and the numerous events associated with it have inspired people of faith since the days when Abraham left his home in Ur (southern Iraq today) and followed God's call to the "promised land." The very mention of this sacred city calls forth a variety of images as well as feelings of personal and corporate identity among the two and one-half billion people around the world who follow the Jewish, Christian and Islamic religious traditions.

The Jewish Holy City   Jerusalem is mentioned more than 650 times in the Hebrew Scriptures. The city was built around Mount Moriah, the site where Abraham was prepared to sacrifice his son according to God's command. One has only to read the biblical accounts of David and Solomon, or the great prophets — Isaiah, Jeremiah, Micah and others — to grasp the importance of Jerusalem in Jewish history. The Psalmist expresses the close attachment to Jerusalem in the words of a people in exile:

> By the rivers of Babylon —
>   there we sat down and there we wept
>   when we remembered Zion.
> On the willows there
>   we hung up our harps.
> For there our captors
>   asked us for songs,   .
> and our tormentors asked for mirth, saying,
>   "Sing us one of the songs of Zion!"
> How could we sing the Lord's song
>   in a foreign land?
> If I forget you, O Jerusalem,
>   let my right hand wither!

Let my tongue cling to the roof of my mouth,
   if I do not remember you,
if I do not set Jerusalem above my highest joy.
                                    (Psalm 137:1–6)

Rooted in biblical history, the special place of Jerusalem in Jewish life and tradition is as vibrant today as it has ever been. Jerusalem permeates the ritual life of Judaism. After every meal the prayer includes a reference to Jerusalem: "Please, O Lord, have mercy upon us, upon Israel, Thy people, and upon Jerusalem, Thy city. Build Jerusalem, the Holy City, speedily in our days." According to Jewish law, Jews should face in the direction of Jerusalem when praying. Twice a year, at the close of the Passover seder and at the close of the service of Yom Kippur (Day of Atonement), the most holy day in the Jewish calendar, Jews utter the deep desire of the heart: "Next year in Jerusalem!"

For most Jews, this frequently repeated hope took on new life when the modern state of Israel was established in 1948. The 1967 war marked the next phase in the unfolding drama. The decisive military victory over Egypt and its Arab allies united the divided city under Israeli control. Jerusalem's continuing religious and political importance for the Jewish community is evident in the daily news. One has only to listen to the concerns and pronouncements of Israeli and American Jewish leaders to perceive the connection.

City of the Farthest Mosque   Jerusalem is also central in Islamic history. Living in a predominantly Christian culture, however, most North Americans know very little about the Islamic perspective. After Mecca and Medina, Jerusalem is the third most sacred site for Muslims. The Arabic name for the city is *al-quds*, meaning "the holy place." In addition to its connection with biblical figures — people who are also revered in Islam — *al-quds* is the site where Muhammad, the prophet of Islam, is believed to have been transported miraculously by God on a special "night journey." From Jerusalem, Muslims affirm, Muhammad was taken up into heaven for a vision of paradise. The site of the Temple of Solomon in Jerusalem took on added significance for Muslims as the location of the "farthest mosque." The Qur'an describes these special events in this passage:

Glory be to Him, who carried His servant by night.
From the holy mosque [Mecca] to the farthest mosque.

The precincts of which We have blessed.
That We might show him [Muhammad] of Our signs.
He [God] is the All-Hearing, the All-Seeing.

(Qur'an 17:1)*

For almost two years after Muhammad's unique religious experience, Muslims were instructed to orient themselves toward Jerusalem during the five daily prayers. Later, the sacred mosque in Mecca, the Ka'bah, replaced Jerusalem as the point of orientation. Even so, Jerusalem has remained particularly revered by Muslims throughout the centuries.

Within a decade of Muhammad's death (632 C.E.†), Muslims had conquered Jerusalem. While the physical control of the city has shifted from time to time, a substantial Muslim community has resided there since the seventh century. Today, two impressive Islamic structures are prominent within the sacred precincts of the old city: the Dome of the Rock sits majestically over the rock from which Muhammad is thought to have ascended for his vision of heaven, and al-aqsa ("the farthest") mosque is nearby, located above the hallowed Western Wall.

The City of Jesus The importance of Jerusalem for Christians is well-known. Christians, who also share in the rich heritage of the Hebrew Scriptures, associate Jerusalem with a number of places and events during the final week of Jesus' life: the Mount of Olives, Palm Sunday, the Last Supper, the Garden of Gethsemane, the stations of the cross, the crucifixion at Golgotha and resurrection from the tomb.

Each year, hundreds of thousands of tourists and pilgrims travel to the Holy Land to visit the biblical sites. A particularly festive and moving celebration occurs annually when Jesus' triumphal entry into Jerusalem is reenacted on Palm Sunday. Several thousand Christians from all parts of the world and all denominations join the march

---

*The translation from the Arabic is by the author. Several English versions of the Qur'an are readily available in many bookstores. These include *The Meaning of the Glorious Koran,* by Muhammad M. Pickthall; *The Koran,* by A.J. Arberry; and *The Holy Qur'an,* by Yusuf Ali.

†C.E. stands for "common era." In place of the traditional designations B.C. and A.D.," most writers are now using "B.C.E." ("before the common era") and "C.E." This enables Christians, Muslims, Jews, Hindus and others to retain standard Western dates without specific reference to Christianity.

down the Mount of Olives and into the old city. Along the route, part-way down the Mount of Olives, the pilgrims pass *Dominus Flevit*, the chapel commemorating the site where Jesus paused as he approached Jerusalem:

> As he came near and saw the city, he wept over it, saying, "If you, even you, had only recognized on this day the things that make for peace! But now they are hidden from your eyes."
>
> (Luke 19:41–42)

As they look from the chapel out over the city of Jerusalem, the poignancy of Jesus' experience comes alive for those who long for justice and peace today. The ancient and the contemporary mingle in a powerful, if unsettling way. Most pilgrims cannot escape the trauma and tragedy experienced by the Jews, Christians and Muslims who, linked by the strong bonds of sacred history, currently inhabit this city and the lands of this region.

The Media Barrage

The deep connection with the Middle East that is rooted in religious history is often overshadowed by our reactions to the more visible and volatile events dominating news from the Middle East. This is hardly surprising, since we are bombarded continually with media images and brief "sound bite" explanations of momentous developments. Predictably, the media focus almost always falls on the dramatic, the sensational and the violent.

Simplistic Images   The barrage of television images often perpetuates negative stereotypes. Iranians, Iraqis, Turks, Lebanese, Kurds, even Israelis are portrayed in caricature, often in relation to a conflict. Rarely, for instance, are the extremist words and actions of Jewish settlers in the Occupied West Bank placed in the larger context of the Israeli society. How often do we see and hear from the large body of Israelis who oppose the settlement policies? Or from leaders in the Israeli Arab community? The Israeli Arabs, Palestinians who remained inside Israel proper in 1948 and became citizens, number over 700,000. Yet they are hardly visible in the extensive media coverage of the region.

Stereotypes also abound in relation to the broader Arab and Muslim communities. Terms like "Arab," "Muslim" and "Iranian" are used almost interchangeably in the popular press. News cover-

The photograph above shows the Dome of the Rock and the old city of Jerusalem viewed from the chapel, Dominus Flevit, the site where Jesus wept as he surveyed Jerusalem from the Mount of Olives. (Photo by James M. Pitts)

The Western Wall (below), the hallowed site in Judaism today, is what remains from the destruction of the Temple in 70 C.E. The original temple complex was completed by King Solomon 3000 years ago. (WCC photo: Peter Williams)

age that focuses on turbulent events often reinforces highly negative images. Without question, the misguided actions of a truck
bomber, an airline hijacker, a terrorist or even the harsh words of
a defiant Arab leader strengthen the longstanding Western bias that
Arabs and Muslims are somehow inherently violent and menac-
ing. We see and hear little of the vast majority of Arabic-speaking
people. Where are the portraits of the tens of millions of Arabs
who get up in the morning, work for a living, seek to educate
and raise children — people facing the familiar challenges and anxieties of daily life? Rarely do we see Arabs as normal human beings
who are as horrified by the behavior of violent extremists as most
North American Christians are by the violent actions of extremists
in Northern Ireland.

The highly audible rhetoric of Saddam Hussein during the Gulf
crisis and war of 1990–91 illustrates how the pattern often works.
Saddam Hussein had ruled Iraq with an iron fist for more than a
decade before he launched the ill-fated assault on neighboring Kuwait. When his behavior appeared to threaten the flow of oil and
thereby global economic stability, the whole world snapped to attention. His subsequent political and religious rhetoric, designed to elicit
support from wherever he could get it, was featured daily in the media. So, too, was detailed information on Iraq's dismal human rights
record under the Iraqi regime. The fact that some Arabs responded
to some elements of his rhetoric added to the negative and simplistic
portrayal. When most of what they hear builds on a long history of
fear and misunderstanding of Arabs, it is not surprising that many
people translate these snapshot images into broader stereotypes of
Middle Easterners, especially Arabs and Muslims.

Prior to the 1990–91 crisis, only a few people in the West knew
anything about Iraq — except that the country had been locked in a
bloody war of attrition with Iran throughout the 1980s. Under the
scrutiny of intense international media attention, we began to learn
more. Iraq, it turns out, is located in the ancient cradle of civilization, the land where the Tigris and Euphrates rivers flow. It was from
this area that Abraham set forth to seek the promised land. The ancient city of Babylon is also located within Iraq. Saddam Hussein's
much-publicized efforts to restore Babylon to its splendor and his
self-characterization as the new Nebuchadnezzar provoked considerable response in Western religious circles. Nebuchadnezzar was the
king whose armies destroyed Jerusalem in 587–86 B.C.E. and then
carried off the Jewish people into exile in Babylon.

WHO IS AN ARAB?

It is not easy to define accurately the term "Arab." The British geographer W. B. Fisher, in his book *The Middle East: A Physical, Social and Regional Geography,* states: "From the point of view of the anthropologist, it is impossible to speak with accuracy either of an Arab or of a Semitic people. Both terms connote a mixed population varying widely in physical character and in racial origin, and are best used purely as cultural and linguistic terms, respectively." Thus the so-called Arab countries are those that share a common culture and speak Arabic as the primary language.

As Islam spread from the Arabian Peninsula there took place Arabization and Islamization—processes that are closely linked but not identical. Peter Mansfield writes in *The Arabs: A Comprehensive History* that "Arabization began some two centuries before the Prophet Muhammad, with the overflow of Arabian tribes into Syria and Iraq, and reached its greatest impulse during the first decades of the Arab Empire. Islamization lasted much longer and still continues today, especially in Africa."

The Arab countries are Egypt, Syria, Jordan, Lebanon, Iraq, Saudi Arabia, North and South Yemen, Kuwait, Bahrain, Oman, Qatar, a loose group of tiny sheikdoms on the Persian Gulf that form the United Arab Emirates, and the North African countries collectively known as the Maghreb—Morocco, Algeria, Tunisia, and Libya.

Islam is the predominant religion today in all of these countries. That in itself, however, does not define an Arab nation. Turkey, Iran, Afghanistan, Pakistan, Indonesia, the Sudan, and Somalia are Islamic, but not Arab. Similarly, not all Arabs are Moslems. Lebanon's population includes close to a million Arab Christians. In several other Middle Eastern countries there are significant Arab Christian minorities—some with ancestral roots antedating the Moslem conquests and others converted by missionaries. There are also several non-Arab Moslem minorities in the Middle East, including the Kurds in parts of Iraq, Iran, and Turkey.

Reprinted from The Middle East, *7th ed. (Washington, D.C.: Congressional Quarterly, Inc., 1990), p. 11. Used by permission.*

Detailed Ignorance   When these images were coupled with Iraq's repeated attacks on the modern state of Israel — with SCUD missiles and hostile rhetoric — current events were again juxtaposed with biblical places and events. For many Western Christians, particularly those on the more conservative to fundamentalist end of the theological spectrum, the perceived links between biblical passages and current events were the most important parts of the international crisis. Numerous television preachers echoed a common theme: these events point this generation toward the final conflagration, the battle of Armageddon. In the U.S. and Canada, several million books, video cassettes and audio tapes were sold to people eager to understand the momentous events in the light of this type of biblical interpretation. Many of these resources must now be modified or revamped entirely since, at least in the short run, the events did not play into an anticipated Armageddon scenario.

For most North American Christians, however, the flood of images and pieces of information did not produce a clearer understanding either of prophetic writings or of current political machinations. Rather, the details created a confusing array in which current events swirled together with names and places from our religious history. Such confusion also arises out of the coverage of and responses to the ongoing clashes in Israel/Palestine and Lebanon.

The confusion does not necessarily temper the ways most North American Christians feel about situations in the Middle East or express their views on events there. Try an experiment. The next time a dramatic development or violent incident in the Middle East grabs the headlines, take an informal survey among friends and colleagues. Ask them how they feel about the event. You will likely discover that few people are indifferent or dispassionate. Continue your probe by asking people to put the incident into context: How does that particular development relate to larger sets of issues? How can we, as concerned citizens in Canada or the U.S., contribute constructively toward resolving the longstanding problems plaguing the region? In most instances, these latter questions will produce very different types of responses from those describing what people feel about a particular situation.

Strong feelings about isolated events are rarely coupled with coherent understanding of issues or measured analysis of what we might do to help. Instead, we may well be caught in detailed ignorance. We know a lot of details, but far too often we remain ignorant about the broader context, at a loss for how to make sense of the specifics. Concerned people of faith in North America can and must address this problem constructively. The challenge is formidable. There are no easy answers. But for people who care deeply about peace and justice there are ways to make substantial contributions toward a more hopeful future. We start when we recognize our particular relationships and responsibilities as Christians in North America.

Our Christian Bonds

Christians are drawn to events in the Middle East by at least four sets of interests. We have already noted the first of these, namely, the strong religious and emotional ties rooted in the history of the Middle East. Second, we must consider the special responsibilities we bear as Christians in and citizens of the United States and Canada. The actions of our governments — be they constructive or detrimental — directly affect the lives of people in the Middle East. The point was illustrated for me one evening in October 1988. In the month before the U.S. presidential election, a Palestinian Christian was addressing a church audience. At one point he was asked which presidential candidate he, as a Palestinian, thought would be most helpful in pursuing Middle East peace. I was surprised by his response, which included these words (here paraphrased):

> Sometimes I feel that you do not appreciate how fortunate you are. Not only do you have your own country, but you also enjoy a democratic system. We in the Middle East are always amazed when we learn how few people vote in major elections. We Palestinians yearn for the day when we can vote openly on issues in our own homeland. For now, I think all Middle Easterners ought to be allowed to vote in the U.S. presidential elections. Why? Because we feel the impact of your government's decisions directly every day. I suspect we feel it more directly than many of you who live here do!

We often forget that our systems of government not only allow participation by the citizenry, they require participation. As citizens in democratic societies, we share responsibility for what is said and done in our name. Since Christians are by far the largest religious group in Canada and the U.S., what we think, say and do — or what we fail to think, say and do — may have a substantial impact on the debate within our society and the policy decisions by our government officials. To fulfill our responsibility we need to inform ourselves and find effective means to communicate our concerns to those who represent us in government. North American Christians cannot solve the daunting problems permeating the Middle East. But we do have the opportunity and obligation to make a substantial contribution as citizens whose countries' acts will affect the course of events.

The Christian Vocation   The third compelling reason to deal with the issues and work constructively for peace comes from our Christian vocation. Christians are far from united on precisely what faith requires in a given situation. Most agree, however, that it is important for Christians to be pastoral, prophetic and reconciling in human society. Our behavior must be shaped in light of thoughtful, prayerful and honest involvement with the issues. The pursuit of this vocation does not allow for silence or avoiding differences.

The Middle East certainly qualifies as a region for focused efforts at reconciliation. While conflict and turmoil are tragic realities in various areas of the world, nowhere is the need for stability greater than in the Middle East. The economic, political and religious importance of this region was clear during the Gulf crisis of 1990–91. The unpredictable swings in the world's stock markets in the weeks following Iraq's invasion of Kuwait testified to how interdependent the world's economic structures are. Events in the Middle East continue to reverberate throughout the world.

The pursuit of peace and stability in the Middle East took on new urgency in the months after the Gulf war. Concerted efforts to find viable peace processes were motivated both by a concern for the people caught in the cycles of violence and by the realization that war and instability in the Middle East spell trouble for everyone who shares this fragile planet.

In fact, the Middle East is a microcosm of the larger world, showing that religious, political and cultural diversities are realities just as much as pluralism and interdependence are. Simply stated, the challenge is this: either we all find new ways to live together with our diversity or we may not live at all. The relationships in the tiny nation of Lebanon serve as a striking example.

As Lebanon Goes, So Goes the World   Throughout most of the twentieth century, Lebanon has been a symbol of peaceful coexistence in a multireligious, largely democratic society. The various Christian and Muslim communities that constitute the diverse population have always been roughly comparable in size. However, the government system bequeathed to Lebanon by the departing French colonial leaders in 1942 accorded disproportionate power to the Maronite Christian community. In the past two decades, the demographic balance has shifted and the Muslims now constitute the majority. Failure to remedy widely perceived political and economic inequities has undermined the cooperative system. Since the mid-1970s, Lebanon has been embroiled in a multisided civil war fed by numerous outside interests.

Although the conflict did not begin as antagonism between religious communities, the political and economic polarization soon divided many along religious lines. The divisions deepened as the horrors and atrocities of war took a devastating toll among both soldiers in the various militias and civilians.

Throughout the years of bitter strife, most Lebanese continued to insist that they wanted to rebuild their multireligious society in a way that respected the rights of all communities. There are hopeful signs in the early 1990s that Lebanon could still emerge from this long nightmare and perhaps even become a model for other pluralist societies. As Christians, we are called to nurture these hopes through prayer and whatever efforts we can devote to the process. The concern includes but also goes beyond the region. If the Lebanese cannot find a way to live together with their diversity, it will not bode well for the rest of the region or, for that matter, the rest of the world.

Ecumenical Links   Finally, Christians in North America are drawn to the Middle East through ecumenical relationships. We are linked directly with the Christian community that lives, worships and bears witness to the gospel in the same lands where the church was born. Regrettably, the very existence of the contemporary Middle Eastern Christian community remains a well-kept secret in the West. Most North American Christians have very little idea who the Middle Eastern Christians are, the size of their churches or the varieties of ministry they practice in their respective situations.

For the past four decades, regional and international ecumenical groupings — most notably councils of churches — have established and nurtured relationships between churches in North America and those in the Middle East. As with ecumenical relationships in other parts of the world, Christians seek to share their hopes, dreams, fears and concerns in mutuality. From a theological perspective, the church is one. When one part of the body of Christ is in pain or turmoil, the whole body shares in that pain. So it is with the part of the body that comprises the Middle East churches. As sisters and brothers in Christ, we must seek to understand their pain, learn from their wisdom and experience and explore ways we can provide assistance. The call to mutual ministry within the church universal means we need to be involved with the people, churches and problems present in the Middle East.

As we have seen, several kinds of concerns draw North American Christians to the Middle East. The challenges and opportunities growing out of these ties call for responses at several levels. Our call to mutual mission with our sisters and brothers in the Middle Eastern churches includes intentional efforts to get to know one another, fortify relationships and consciously cooperate in ministry. At the same time, we should seek to understand the major issues affecting all people and shaping events in that turbulent region. We must also consider carefully our particular responsibilities as citizens. As we pay thoughtful attention and make responsible efforts to be engaged in these various dimensions of ministry, we can discover constructive ways to move forward in mutual ministry and as responsible citizens.

Before we explore the opportunities and challenges in more detail, we begin by looking back. The dynamics that we see operating in the Middle East today, particularly those within the churches, are rooted in the unique histories of these lands. While Christians in the Middle East and the West are now finding their way together in unprecedented ways, we need to keep in mind the different historical experiences that bring us to this juncture. A brief overview of Middle Eastern church history will orient us for the remainder of our study. It provides a frame of reference for understanding how Middle Eastern churches are organized and related to one another. It also establishes a backdrop against which we can interpret the current events in this region.

A BRIEF HISTORY OF THE CHURCHES

Most Middle Eastern churches trace their origins to the apostolic era. The New Testament portrays Paul as the zealous missionary whose extensive travels established churches in various parts of the Mediterranean world. Although we cannot know the precise history, longstanding church traditions associate various other disciples and first-century Christians with the spread of the gospel from Palestine as well: Peter (and Paul) ventured west to Rome, the heart of the Roman Empire; Mark is revered in Egypt for having brought the "good news"; Thomas is believed to have gone east and established churches in ancient Mesopotamia (present-day Iraq) as well as India; Barnabas is identified with the founding of the church on the island nation of Cyprus.

From humble beginnings, the Christian community multiplied rapidly in the first three centuries. The growth produced controversies as new issues surfaced and people of faith differed in their responses. Through the later New Testament texts and some extant writings of church leaders, we know a good deal about the rich diversity of views on issues of doctrine and polity during this formative period. The primacy of certain bishops and the authority of selected writings helped define the debates. But the content of the New Testament, the canon as we now accept it, was not fixed until the end of the fourth century. And even after the debate over what books belonged in the Bible was decided, the process of theological reflection and clarification remained an ongoing task.

The vigor and tenacity of these early Christians were manifest in hardships they faced. The challenges presented by internal disputes and doctrinal differences were compounded by the turbulent political situation. For many followers of Jesus, the way of the cross included the experience of persecution. But despite physical danger and doctrinal differences, the community of believers flourished and continued to spread.

By the third century, institutional structures and patterns of authority were becoming more clearly established. Geographically, the church was divided into areas of jurisdiction. The principal seat of authority was called a see. There were four major sees in the early church. The leader with primary authority over the bishops and churches in a see was called the patriarch. Three of the four major centers of Christian ecclesiastical authority were in the area we call the Middle East today: Alexandria (in Egypt), Antioch (in Syria), and Jerusalem. The fourth great center was Rome. The churches in the contemporary Middle East continue to relate to the structures of these ancient patriarchates.

Constantine and Nicea

In the early decades of the fourth century, the situation for most Christians changed dramatically when Constantine became Emperor of the Roman Empire. Inspired by the Christian message and the faith of his Christian mother, Helena, Constantine reversed the fortunes of the church by showing imperial favor for Christianity and proclaiming toleration for all religions. Now, the religious community that had sought protection from persecution and distinction from pagan practices assumed a new role, namely, the dominant religion in the empire.

Helena, who was later proclaimed a saint, made a distinctive contribution to the church. Her strong sense of attachment to the Holy Land led her to travel there and endeavor to locate the sites — in Bethlehem, Nazareth, Jerusalem — where major events in Jesus' life were thought to have occurred. Churches were then constructed on these traditional sites and making pilgrimages to worship at them soon became an honored way to practice Christian piety.

From the time of Constantine forward, the once-powerful Roman Empire entered a period of decline. Various "barbarians" besieged and even conquered portions of the empire. Concerns over political fragmentation and instability were factors prompting Constantine to seek to resolve the growing disputes among church leaders. These efforts became one of Constantine's most enduring legacies.

Contending parties appealed to him to settle differences. In 325, he summoned church leaders to Nicea to seek agreement in the theological controversies surrounding the nature of the Trinity. This remarkable gathering was the first of the seven great ecumenical councils. These gatherings were called "ecumenical" because they included church leaders and representatives from "the whole inhabited earth" (the meaning of the Greek word *oikumene*).* The deliberations of some 318 church fathers resulted in the Nicene Creed, the doc-

---

*Most substantial church history texts include detailed analysis of these major formative councils. See, for instance, Jaroslav Pelikan, *The Christian Tradition: A History of the Development of Doctrine*, 5 vols. (Chicago: University of Chicago Press, 1971–89).

trinal affirmation that proclaims the Father, Son and Holy Spirit to be "three persons, one substance."

The origins of the Middle Eastern churches can be traced to theological differences debated vigorously during the major ecumenical councils of these early centuries. These early divisions were by no means unique in church history. Similar patterns of schism can be traced through the centuries. The bewildering array of hundreds of Christian denominations today bears witness to this phenomenon. Differences in theological understanding, doctrinal formulation and organizing church polity continue to produce new denominations on the eve of the third millennium of the church.

The Split at Chalcedon

Following Nicea, councils were held in Constantinople (381) and Ephesus (431). Each of these both condemned certain bishops for heretical teachings and further clarified which doctrinal formulations were regarded by the majority as orthodox. In 431, Nestorius, Bishop of Constantinople, was declared a heretic for teaching that two distinct persons — one human and one divine — were present in the incarnate Christ. He rejected the term *theotokos* (God-bearer), the designation the majority favored for the Virgin Mary. Subsequently, Nestorius and his followers moved further east, forming the nucleus of what would become the Assyrian Church of the East.

A decisive split occurred in 451 during the Council of Chalcedon. Reaffirming earlier positions, this ecumenical grouping of more than 500 bishops debated different perspectives on the two natures of Christ. In the end, they declared the human and divine natures to be united "unconfusedly, unchangeably, indivisibly, and inseparably." Those Christians who favored an emphasis on the single, divine nature of Christ (the Monophysites) were effectively severed from the larger community. In the two centuries following Chalcedon, the advocates of the Monophysite position formed the three great Oriental Orthodox churches: Coptic, Syrian and Armenian. For more than fifteen centuries, these communities have continued their witness and ministry as independent, self-governing (often called "autocephalous," that is, "self-headed") churches.

These churches constitute the majority Christian community in the Middle East today. And, happily, they are finding their way back together with other Orthodox, Catholic and Protestant Christians through common ministry in the Middle East Council of Churches.

The other main grouping of Orthodox churches, called the Eastern Orthodox, were those who embraced the Chalcedonian position and remained in communion with the bishop of Rome for six more centuries. Their history and development are related to the political patterns within the Mediterranean world.

Constantine transferred the administrative center of the Roman Empire to Constantinople. From 363 onward, however, there were almost always two Roman Emperors: one ostensibly (though not always physically) based in Rome, one in Constantinople. There was a good deal of cooperation and collaboration between the two halves of the Roman Empire. The Eastern realm is often called the Byzantine Empire, since Byzantium was the earlier name for Constantinople. Although this center of the empire began with the Latin-speaking heritage of Rome, it soon became assimilated into the Greek culture. That heritage has continued up to the present day, with several major churches grouped under the heading "Eastern Orthodox," most notably the Greek Orthodox Church, the Russian Orthodox Church and the Church of Cyprus.

The Expansion of Islam

The appearance and rapid spread of Islam in the seventh century dramatically changed the historic lands of early Christendom. Within two decades of Muhammad's death in Arabia in 632 C.E., Muslims had effective control of Jerusalem, Damascus and Alexandria. In the short space of one century, Islam transformed the character and culture of lands from northern India through the Fertile Crescent across North Africa and into Spain. In the process, the unity of the Mediterranean world was disrupted and the axis of Christendom shifted to the north.

Contrary to the image popular in the West, Muslims did not simply roar out of the Arabian desert, plunder everything in sight and force conversions by the sword. The expansion of Islam, unprecedented in scope, was a multifaceted phenomenon. At that time, the political situation in the eastern part of the Roman Empire was tenuous at best. The western half of the empire had already lost most of its power. Considerable friction, at times outright hostility, characterized the relationships between many of the Oriental (Syriac and Coptic) Orthodox churches and their political Byzantine rulers in Constantinople. In several settings, Christians appear to have offered little resistance to the Muslim conquerors or even welcomed them.

Diverse political and religious factors were at work in this turbulent period. Many people were anxious for political change; they were happy to get the oppressive Byzantine rulers off their backs. In addition, Islam was not always perceived as an entirely new or necessarily threatening religious system.

In fact, the first coherent treatment of Islam and the Arab conquest we have from that period considers Islam not as an alien tradition but as a kind of Christian heresy. John of Damascus, a great Christian thinker and theologian who died around 750, was raised near the military and administrative center of Islam, which had moved from Mecca to Damascus. John found much in the Qur'an and the Muslim community that was compatible with the Bible: one God, creator of the universe; human responsibility to worship God and serve the community; the certainty of judgment; heaven and hell; and deep reverence for such biblical figures as Noah, Abraham, Moses, David, John the Baptist and Jesus.

At the same time, the Qur'an and Islamic teachings posed major theological problems: they rejected the divinity of Christ and the doctrine of the Trinity. Jesus' virgin birth was affirmed, but the Qur'an made clear that God has no "sons"; the crucifixion was acknowledged, but the resurrection was denied. John of Damascus, and many other Christians after him, struggled with issues like these even as they found ways to live side-by-side with their Muslim neighbors.

Checkered Relationships

Islam changed the complexion of Christianity. Those churches lodged within the Muslim domain became largely isolated from churches in Europe. On the positive side, their new circumstances as minority communities under Islamic rule served to strengthen and solidify their identities.

For many centuries the Islamic empire flourished. The Arab Muslims — in collaboration with Muslims from Persia and Egypt as well as Christians and Jews — produced a civilization remarkably advanced in philosophy, mathematics, medicine, chemistry and horticulture. Within the Islamic domain, Christians and Jews were considered "People of the Book" and, as such, legitimate religious communities deserving "protection" under Islam. They were given limited authority over religious affairs. "Protected" status had its disadvantages, to be sure. Muslims enjoyed decided economic and political advantages in society; Christians and Jews were required to pay higher taxes as protected minorities even as they faced severely limited opportunities for economic advancement. Over time, major segments of the Christian community were assimilated into Islam through intermarriage and conversion. This was particularly true across most of Northern Africa, where the once thriving Christian community virtually disappeared within the first three centuries of Islamic rule.

Relations between Christians, Muslims and Jews through the Middle Ages are not easily characterized. Many factors influenced relationships in different settings over the centuries. Much of the Islamic empire, for example, was conquered in the thirteenth century by Mongol armies coming from the East. The name of powerful Ghengis Khan (died in 1227 C.E.) is forever etched in the history and experience of Muslims, Christians and Jews in Russia, Persia (Iran), Turkey and parts of the Arabic-speaking Middle East. The impact of the Turkish leader Tamerlane (1336–1405 C.E.) was pervasive as well. We cannot generalize about the way traumatic political events affected relationships within and among these religious communities. Careful study of particular times and places is required.

This much is clear: the popular image of the children of Abraham as incompatible, always fighting and killing one another, does not square with reality. For fourteen centuries, they have lived together in the Middle East and Mediterranean region. In the history of the Middle Ages we can find numerous examples of harmonious relations and cooperation as well as recurrent patterns of mutual antipathy and open conflict, especially between Christians and Muslims.* Insofar as the Jewish community experienced conflict, it was usually on the receiving end. The history of Jews facing the Inquisition in Spain (beginning in 1479 C.E.) illustrates the point. By contrast, many Jews in Islamic Spain flourished in the ninth to eleventh centuries.

The Crusades

The greatest fears and harshest critiques of Islam have been expressed most often by people in Western nations rather than by

---

*See Charles Kimball, *Striving Together: A Way Forward in Christian-Muslim Relations* (Maryknoll, N.Y.: Orbis Books, 1991), for an exploration of the history as well as the challenges and opportunities presented by the encounter between Christians and Muslims, the world's two largest religious communities.

those Christians living side-by-side and interacting daily with Muslims. The most dramatic manifestation of Western Christian hostility toward Islam was the Crusades.

The Crusades were launched at the end of the eleventh century (1096), supposedly to recapture the Holy Land from the Muslim "infidels." Several religious and political concerns spurred Europeans to mount eight Crusades over the following two centuries. Beyond the Crusaders' stated zeal to reclaim the holy sites, there were serious tensions between Eastern and Western Christendom in the eleventh century. The Eastern Orthodox and Roman Catholic churches had split formally in 1054 after several centuries of unresolved doctrinal disputes and political struggles between church leaders based in Rome and Constantinople.

The full measure of animosity between Christians at that time is reflected in the suffering the Crusaders inflicted on Eastern Christians during their various expeditions. The Crusaders' zeal to fight Muslims was also felt by the unfortunate Jews whom they encountered. A close study of the Crusades reveals a startling, grim picture, one that includes wholesale slaughter of Jews and a murderous attack on Constantinople.

Although the Crusades are no longer viewed in the West as particularly noble, they did cast a long shadow for many centuries. Medieval writers were inspired by the stories of chivalry and fighting for holy causes. Our Western perceptions of those events, however vague, have been shaped by European literature. But Muslims and most Middle Eastern Christians still live in the shadow of Crusader castles and sites where battles and massacres took place. The collective memory is real, powerful and negative. The 1991 Gulf war provided a view of just how strong these memories are in the Middle East. Several Muslim leaders openly compared the U.S.-led response to Iraq as a "new Crusade" by Western Christians. A major *New York Times* article on February 3, 1991, was headlined, "Bush's Holy War: The Crusader's Cloak Can Grow Heavy on the Shoulders." This rhetoric struck a deep, painful chord for many Middle Easterners.

Foreign Domination

The Byzantine Empire lasted for over a thousand years, until Constantinople fall to the Ottoman Turks in 1453. For the next four centuries, the Ottoman Empire ruled the Middle East. The Ottoman rise to power also marked a turning point for most Middle Eastern Muslims. Although the Ottomans were Muslims, most Muslims and Christians living under Ottoman rule perceived them as a foreign presence motivated not by Islam but by visions of empire. To put it gently, the Ottomans were not concerned primarily with the wishes and best interests of the people under their rule. Yet the Ottomans did provide a degree of stability over a large geographic region. By the nineteenth century their empire was weakening. As it broke apart, European colonial powers moved in and gained control, adding the lands of the Middle East to a larger network in Asia and Africa.

Colonial domination culminated with the Allied victory in World War I. With the complete dissolution of the Ottoman Empire, the British and the French became the primary European powers in the Middle East. Their policies and practices have left an enduring legacy in the region.

The continuing pattern of external domination was humiliating to Middle Easterners. The economic exploitation inherent in colonial rule further angered the Arabs, Iranians, Kurds and others. To help run the lands they controlled, the Europeans often installed hand-picked government leaders. Many people acquiesced to the colonialist powers, particularly if doing so assured them wealth and privilege. The vast majority, who did not benefit tangibly, were all the more embittered. The combination of unrepresentative governments guided by foreign, non-Muslim powers stimulated both religious and political reform movements in various Middle Eastern lands. These reforms continue throughout the Muslim world today. Some of the movements have been especially visible because they employ violent methods to disrupt the political structures and draw attention to their cause.

In many instances, the colonialists also established new national boundaries. These divisions made sense from the perspective of the political and economic interests of the ruling authorities; for the region's inhabitants, however, they were often artificial lines, dividing peoples arbitrarily.

An Ambiguous Legacy

The colonialist presence produced, at best, mixed results for Middle Eastern Christians. On the one hand, Europeans facilitated nineteenth-century missionary efforts. In many cases this meant new opportunities and measurable improvements in areas such as education and health care. On the other hand, many Middle Christians felt negative effects from the influx of Western Christians. In some settings, for example, eager missionaries shifted the primary focus for their endeavors to local churches. This was particularly true in places where the Muslim response to evangelization was minimal.

Like others in their societies, Christians felt the sting of condescending and manipulative behavior predictably present among those with tremendous political and economic power. On the whole, control and exploitation by foreign powers engendered deep animosity in the general populace.

The second half of the twentieth century has witnessed the creation of many new nation-states in the world. Many of the new countries have arisen in the shadow of colonialism and in the midst of civil unrest. The normal pains associated with the birth of new nation-states have been even sharper in the Middle East, where various regional and superpower agendas converge and often conflict. In the midst of this confusion and political transition, the time-honored churches in the Middle East have sought to continue their work and witness in creative, effective ways.

We turn now to a consideration of the work and witness of these churches, equipped with a better understanding of their rich and tumultuous history.

2

Middle Eastern Christians Today

FAMILIES OF CHURCHES

Egypt. The very name invokes pyramids, hieroglyphics, and the river Nile. These images fit well this ancient land of the pharaohs. But there is much more. Biblical history is also woven into the fabric of five thousand years of Egyptian civilization. The book of Genesis includes prominent stories of Abraham's journey to Egypt and Joseph's rise to power there after being sold into slavery by his jealous brothers. The compelling story of Moses — from his infancy to his confrontation with the pharaoh and the exodus of the people of Israel — unfolds in Egypt.

In the New Testament, the Gospel of Matthew tells how Joseph and Mary fled the wrath of King Herod by escaping to Egypt with the newborn Jesus. The story, recorded in Matthew 2:13–23, suggests that the sojourn of the holy family lasted at least two years.

The connection with Egypt continued in the first-century church. As we noted in chapter 1, Mark is revered as the evangelist who brought the message of the gospel to the people of Egypt. His proclamation of the good news was well received. The churches in Egypt took root and grew to the extent that Alexandria became one of the major sees in the early church.

Egyptian churches have continued their worship, witness and

ministry for nearly two thousand years. This rich heritage is alive today in the largest Christian community in the Middle East: the Coptic Orthodox Church. This community of faith is not only one of the oldest churches in the world; it is engaged fully with the challenges of modern life. This blend of the ancient and the contemporary is illustrated in the ministry of a modern-day leader who bears a familiar biblical name, Moses.

Bishop Musa (Arabic for Moses) is the Coptic Orthodox Church's bishop for youth. Before his call to full-time ministry, Bishop Musa was a physician. His desire to serve the church led him to enter the monastery and later become a bishop. For more than a decade he has worked tirelessly with other bishops, priests and local church groups to nurture and develop various youth ministries throughout Egypt. Spending a day with this remarkable man will change your life. His energy, commitment, creativity and hope are contagious. He helps young people understand and appreciate their rich heritage through worship and Bible study. Weekend retreats, weekly social activities and service projects develop fellowship and the sense of community. Other activities, such as educational and vocational training and marriage counseling, help prepare the youth for responsibilities as adults in their overpopulated and very poor country.

The ministry of Bishop Musa provides a glimpse into the life of Middle Eastern churches today. They are very much alive and deeply engaged with ministry in their respective settings. Between ten and twelve million Christians live in the Middle East. The large majority speak Arabic while smaller communities speak Farsi, Armenian or Syriac as their native language and in their worship liturgy. This community of faith is three to four times larger than the Jewish population in Israel. Although a minority within the larger Muslim population, Christians are a significant factor in the societal mix throughout the region.

As Christians in North America awaken to the presence and witness of the Middle Eastern churches, several questions immediately arise. What churches are these? Where exactly do these Christian live? What is their church life like? How are their churches organized? How are they able to pursue their ministry as minority communities in the midst of such political turmoil? What are our responsibilities together with this part of the body of Christ as we seek to serve God and fulfill the mission of the church? Pursuing answers to such questions is the next step in our exploration.

The churches in the Middle East can be grouped into five "families": Oriental Orthodox, Eastern Orthodox, Catholic, Protestant, and the Assyrian Church of the East.* The two largest groupings, by far, are among the Orthodox churches. Approximately 80 percent of the indigenous Christians belong to either Oriental or Eastern Orthodox churches. The Catholic churches account for some 15 percent, while the Protestant churches include roughly 3 to 4 percent of the Middle Eastern Christian community. The Assyrian Church of the East, now dispersed around the world, continues to have worshiping communities in Iraq, Turkey, Syria and Iran.

Collectively, the Middle Eastern Christians represent a 7 to 8 percent minority in the predominantly Muslim region. The relative proportion of Muslims and Christians varies from country to country. Although no accurate figures exist, Lebanon is home for approximately 1.5 million Christians, or about 40 percent of the total population. The numerically largest community is Egypt's six to eight million Copts. Many in the West are surprised to learn that Syria's Christian churches have over one million members. Similarly, more than 400,000 Christians reside in Iraq — a fact that seemed to elude most journalists during the recent Gulf war.

1. Oriental Orthodox Churches

The Oriental Orthodox family includes the Coptic, Armenian and Syrian Orthodox churches. Each of these non-Chalcedonian churches has its distinct history and ethnic identity. Before this century, political and geographical circumstances have kept these independent, self-governing churches relatively isolated from one another as well as from churches outside the region.

The **Coptic Orthodox Church** of Egypt traces its Christian heritage back through St. Mark and its ethnic lineage to the ancient Pharaonic Egyptians. Early Coptic church history is distinguished by the contributions of prominent theologians such as Clement of Alexandria. Egypt also began the practice of monasticism with the

---

*The material included in the following overview of contemporary Middle Eastern churches comes both from the author's ecumenical experience with these churches and from two publications. For a more detailed overview, see Norman Horner, *A Guide to the Churches in the Middle East* (Elkhart, Ind.: Mission Focus Publications, 1989). The second resource, "Who Are the Christians of the Middle East?" *MECC Perspectives* (October 1986), is now out of print.

St. Bishoi Monastery in Wadi Natrorem, Egypt. Photo by Betty Jane Bailey.

From an interview with Anba Musa, Bishop of Youth in the Coptic Church.

In our history, monastic life was never separated from Church life and Church services. We consider monasticism as a complete consecration of the soul to the Lord. Once you are consecrated, you are at His disposal. He may ask you to return back to work. He may ask you to go to a cave and spend your life in prayer. He may ask that you become specialized in certain studies. To my mind, Coptic monasticism has been of a very active kind throughout our history, from the days of St. Anthony, the founder of monasticism. When persecution occurred, St. Anthony came to Alexandria, to strengthen the believers to become steadfast and to die if necessary for the Christian faith. He returned to the monastery when it was over. He came a second time to support St. Athanasios, who was working very hard to fight Arianism. Many monks travelled all over the country and abroad to teach Christianity. We know that some Coptic monks went to Ireland, Switzerland and Asia Minor.

Interview by Youssef Hajjar in WSCF Journal *special issue on the Churches in the Arab World, May 1986.*

third-century desert monastic St. Anthony. Monastic orders continue
to flourish among contemporary Copts.

The head of the Coptic Orthodox Church, the patriarch of Alexandria, bears the title "pope." The current patriarch, Pope Shen-
ouda III, has led the church since 1971. The vibrant leadership
he provides is demonstrated in the popular weekly Bible study he
teaches in Cairo. Visitors are often startled to find over five thousand
people packed into St. Mark's church on Wednesday evenings. They
come to listen to, laugh with and learn from their spiritual leader.

As in other Orthodox churches, the priests are often married; the
bishops, who are all former monks, remain celibate. Lay people are
actively involved in the various ministries throughout the dioceses
in Egypt. During the last century, new dioceses and churches have
been established outside Egypt. There are today 25 congregations in
the U.S., three in Canada and others in many major cities of Europe
and the Middle East.

A large portion of the **Armenian Apostolic Church,** sometimes
called the Armenian Orthodox Church, is based in the Middle East
today. This church traces its origin to the apostolic missionaries Bar-
tholomew and Thaddaeus. The success of their mission makes a
remarkable chapter in church history. The unity and strength of this
church through the centuries have been visible to all: to be an Armenian has always been practically synonymous with being a Christian.
Unfortunately, external relations have been far from harmonious. Armenians, situated originally in lands now governed by the U.S.S.R.
and Turkey, have a long history of political disruption and dispersal.

For over a millennium, Armenians have endured successive on-
slaughts and occupations in their native land. The most recent and
most horrific brutality occurred early this century. Between 1915 and
1922, over 1.5 million Armenians were slaughtered in a genocidal
massacre within Turkey. The survivors were dispersed southward
throughout the Middle East and around the world. Many Westerners remain unaware or only vaguely familiar with the plight of
Armenians, particularly in this century.

The Armenian Orthodox Church is divided into two branches,
one centered in the Soviet Republic of Armenia, the other in Antelias
(Beirut), Lebanon. The Armenians in diaspora relate to one of the
branches. The head of each branch is called the Catholicos. Under
the leadership of Catholicos Karekin II in Beirut, the Armenians in
the Middle East have been among the most active in the twentieth-

century ecumenical movement. During the 1970s and 1980s, Karekin served as one of the presidents of the World Council of Churches and, subsequently, of the Middle East Council of Churches.

The Armenians are among the larger communities in several Middle Eastern lands: 150,000 are in Lebanon; Syria, Iraq and Iran each have Armenian communities of over 100,000. A more visible but smaller community lives and worships within the old city of Jerusalem in the historic "Armenian Quarter."

During the recent Gulf war, the Armenian Bishopric of Iraq was at the forefront of humanitarian efforts to meet the staggering emergency medical and housing needs of civilians caught in the throes of the war. In the months after the fighting ended, the bishopric in Baghdad continued to serve as a focal point for emergency relief efforts among the Iraqi civilian and foreign population.

The third in the Oriental Orthodox family is the **Syrian Orthodox Church**. According to tradition, this church continues the community founded by Peter at Antioch in the year 37 C.E. To this day, members of this church use ancient Syriac in their worship, a language akin to (some say identical with) the Aramaic language spoken by Jesus. The patriarch of Antioch, Mar Ignatius Zakka Iwas, is the head of this community of faith.

The Syrian Orthodox Church is now much smaller than its long and substantial history might suggest. Problems associated with wide dispersion in the region, a major split with the Eastern portion of the church (now resident in India) and the inevitable absorption of immigrants into other churches have all reduced its numbers. Still, some 160,000 Syrian Orthodox, sometimes called Souryanis, gather for worship and witness under the jurisdiction of 26 archbishoprics; 12 are in the Middle East, one serves Canada and the U.S. and two are in South America.

This apostolic church is showing hopeful signs of renewal. On the eve of the twenty-first century, its youth programs are active, and an ambitious effort to build a new seminary in Syria is well underway. The Evangelical Lutheran Church in America has been actively involved in this venture. The image of a new seminary is particularly heartening as one envisions the next generation of church leaders both engaging in contemporary theological education and being equipped to lead the liturgy in the language of Jesus and the disciples.

2. The Eastern (Greek) Orthodox Churches

Six self-governing Eastern Orthodox communions constitute the second major family of churches in the Middle East. Four of these are patriarchates, linked with the ancient centers of Christendom in Constantinople, Antioch, Alexandria and Jerusalem. The two other self-governing churches are in Cyprus and at Mt. Sinai. Though second in membership to the Oriental churches in the Middle East, the Eastern Orthodox churches share a common liturgy and doctrinal history with a much larger Orthodox community worldwide, including many churches more familiar to North American Protestants and Catholics: Russian, Greek, Romanian, Serbian, Polish, Bulgarian, Czechoslovakian, Georgian, and Albanian.

The Eastern Orthodox communions differ from the Oriental churches at two points. First, they embrace the doctrinal statements of the seven ecumenical councils (between 325 and 787); the Oriental churches, as we noted earlier, rejected the creedal formulation at the decisive council of Chalcedon in 451. Second, since the early sixteenth century the Eastern Orthodox churches have recognized the patriarch of Constantinople (now Istanbul) as ecumenical patriarch. In practice, this "first among equals" status is mostly honorary because each church is entirely self-governing.

The **Patriarchate of Constantinople** has jurisdiction over a relatively small community in the Middle East, since few Christians remain in Turkey. Worldwide, however, the patriarch has a wide-ranging authority. The Greek Orthodox Archbishopric of North and South America and the Orthodox churches in most of Western Europe, Australia and New Zealand are within this ecclesiastical jurisdiction.

The largest Eastern Orthodox community in the Middle East is the **Patriarchate of Antioch**. In its liturgy and prayers, this communion uses Arabic, the language of the people. The patriarch, Ignatius IV, resides in Damascus. He, like Catholicos Karekin II in Beirut, has been one of the most active Orthodox leaders in the modern ecumenical movement. He, too, has served a seven-year term as a president of the World Council of Churches. His second full term as a president of the Middle East Council of Churches will expire in 1995.

Some 1.5 million Middle Eastern Christians belong to this ancient church. Over half are in present-day Syria, where they are the largest group of Christians. Almost one-half million are in Lebanon, while more than 30,000 faithful live in Iraq and Kuwait. Interestingly, the authority of this patriarchate extends to some one million Arabic-speaking Orthodox Christians who live and worship in Canada, the U.S. and Latin America today.

The Greek Orthodox **Patriarch of Jerusalem** presides over the Arab Christians of Palestine and Jordan. Traditionally, the leadership for this church has come from Greece. Thus the community reflects a blend of Arabic and Greek heritage, including the use of both languages in worship. Western pilgrims and tourists to the Holy Land frequently have some interaction with this church because it has a major role and responsibility in the care and maintenance of holy places. Unfortunately, most visitors never venture beyond the traditional holy sites to meet the contemporary Palestinian Arab Christians who live and worship in the very places where Jesus once lived.

The **Patriarchate of Alexandria** is on the Egyptian coast. This Arabic-speaking community of believers is today quite small, numbering only about 10,000 in Egypt and across North Africa. The jurisdiction of this patriarchate, however, extends throughout Africa, where an additional 100,000 Orthodox believers live in Kenya, Zaire, Zimbabwe and South Africa.

The **Church of Cyprus** has clear ties to several apostles, according to the New Testament writings. Paul, Barnabas and Mark are mentioned in connection with this beautiful Mediterranean island. Christianity in Cyprus has been strong and constant since the first century. Bishops from Cyprus were present in all the ecumenical councils. At Ephesus in 431, the Church of Cyprus was recognized as autocephalous (self-governing).

The Church of Cyprus has received considerable visibility in the West in recent decades, primarily because of the political unrest plaguing the island. The former leader of the church, Archbishop Makarios, was also a major political actor and thus highly prominent on the world stage. The current head of the church, Archbishop Chrysostomos, though a highly regarded leader, has not been in the forefront politically.

Since the Turkish invasion of 1974, this island nation has been

divided, with the Turkish Cypriot minority living in the north and
the Greek Cypriots in the south. Repeated and concerted efforts
through the offices of the United Nations General Secretariat have
produced hopeful signs that this conflict may be resolved in the
not-too-distant future.

Cyprus, especially the Greek Cypriot region, is unique in the
Middle East as the one place people from various countries have
been able to come together. One finds Israelis, Palestinians, Lebanese
of varying political persuasions, Syrians, Egyptians, Jordanians and
others moving about freely, even meeting with one another. Political issues complicating travel and interaction are not a major
problem here. Cyprus has proven to be an especially important
gathering place for Middle Eastern Christians working ecumenically.
The generous support of the Church of Cyprus — in providing both
physical facilities and resources — has been invaluable for the larger
community of Christians.

Remarkably few North American Christians visiting the Middle
East go to Cyprus. Admittedly, it takes some planning and involves
additional expense since it is off the heavily traveled tourist itineraries. But, as many Europeans know, Cyprus is both a beautiful
island and a delightful place to discover the rich history of a church
rooted in the first century.

Finally, the **Church of Mt. Sinai** is unique among the Eastern
Orthodox. It began with the construction of a monastery complex
in the sixth century. Like other communities in the Middle East, it
has been affected by various wars and conquests. For the most part,
however, this small church has continued in relative isolation. Even
now, it has very little interaction with other Middle Eastern churches.
Even so, it is well-known in scholarly circles today because of its
famous library of ancient Bibles, manuscripts and icons.

3. The Catholic Churches

The family of Middle Eastern Catholic churches is hardly known
in the West. It includes a fascinating mix of seven different communions joined by their affirmation of the spiritual primacy of the pope
in Rome. Sometimes called "uniate" churches, these Catholic bodies
are united to Rome and, at the same time, continue to follow their
distinctive "rites" or liturgical and canon law traditions. An example
of the distinction is the marital status of clergy. As in the Orthodox

Churches of the Middle East

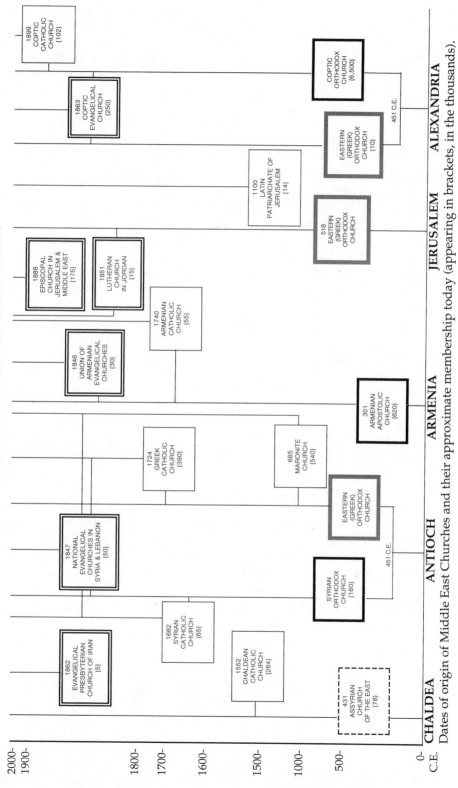

Dates of origin of Middle East Churches and their approximate membership today (appearing in brackets, in the thousands).

churches from which most uniate churches were formed, the priests in these Catholic churches are usually married. The bishops, on the other hand, are selected from the monastic orders and thus practice celibacy.

The oldest and largest Catholic group in the area is the **Maronite Church** in Lebanon. There is some debate among scholars about the date this church began. The Maronites traditionally trace their origin to the fourth or fifth century; others suggest that the church was not identifiable as such until several centuries later. In any event, by the ninth century, Maronites were established in the mountainous terrain of Lebanon. Other groups — Christians, Muslims and Druze (an offshoot of Islam) — have also found safe haven in the mountains during turbulent periods over the centuries. This pattern of seeking refuge accounts in large part for the unique demographic configuration in Lebanon today.

The Maronites formally united with Rome in the twelfth century. The relationship has remained close over the centuries although the Maronites exercise considerable autonomy. They elect their own patriarch and bishops, and they maintain an Eastern rite that derives from the ancient Syriac tradition of Antioch. The current patriarch, Mar Nasrallah Boutros Sfeir, resides in Bkerke, north of Beirut. He has been one of the more visible Middle Eastern Christian leaders in the Western media because of his repeated efforts during the 1980s to intervene and stop the relentless fighting between factions in Lebanon.

The Maronites in Lebanon number more than one million, making them the largest of the many Christian churches in the tiny land. Because of their size and particularly close relations with the French colonialists who governed earlier this century, the Maronites have dominated Lebanon's political scene. The long-outdated census of 1932, which established the Maronites as the largest confessional community in Lebanon, provides the basis for allocating parliamentary seats. Since Lebanon's independence in 1943, the Lebanese have been locked into a structure of leadership defined along religious lines: the president of the country must be a Maronite Christian; the prime minister a Sunni Muslim; and the speaker of the parliament a Shi'ite Muslim. This structure, together with the economic power that derives from political power, is at the center of the conflict in Lebanon. There is widespread agreement on the need for reform, but the precise formula remains to be worked out.

The large majority of Maronites now live outside Lebanon. While the actual figures are elusive, well over five million reside in Europe, Australia, North and South America as well as parts of Africa and elsewhere in the Middle East.

The **Latin Patriarchate of Jerusalem** is the second oldest Catholic church in the region. This community, established at the end of the eleventh century, has shared the upheavals and changing fortunes of the sacred city. For centuries, this church provided the framework for Roman Catholic mission efforts, which led to the establishment of various uniate churches.

Following the Latin rite, the churches under this patriarch are tied directly to Rome. Many of the more than 100,000 Christians worshiping today in Latin-rite churches are expatriates (Americans, Italians, French and other non-Middle Easterners) living and working in Middle Eastern cities such as Cairo, Beirut and Aleppo. The church also includes many Palestinian Christians, most notably in Jerusalem, Bethlehem and Nazareth. In an unprecedented move to affirm the patriarchate of Jerusalem as an indigenous church, Pope John Paul II named Michael Sabbagh the first Palestinian Arab patriarch in 1988.

The **Chaldean Catholic Church** is the third oldest and third largest Middle Eastern Catholic community. Founded in the mid-sixteenth century, this church was formed out of the Assyrian Church of the East (see page 17). The term "Chaldean" has long been associated with the Assyrian churches because they have been largely centered in the ancient area of Chaldea (Babylon). The head of the church is called Patriarch of Babylon. The incumbent patriarch, Paul II Cheikho, resides in Baghdad today.

Approximately half of the 250,000 Chaldean Catholics remain in the Middle East. The large majority of these, perhaps 100,000, form one of Iraq's largest Christian communities. Smaller groupings live in Iran, Syria and Lebanon. A substantial number (80,000) have settled in Canada and the U.S. during the past century.

The **Greek Catholic Church** traces its origin to the early eighteenth century. This Eastern-rite community was formed out of the Eastern Orthodox churches within the Patriarchates of Alexandria, Antioch and Jerusalem. They forged a union with Rome and elected their first patriarch in 1724. The current leader of the church, Maximos V Hakim, bears the title Greek Catholic Patriarch of Antioch, Alexandria and Jerusalem. He now resides in Damascus.

The term "Melkite" is often used in relation to Greek Catholics. It derives from a fifth-century term meaning "the King's men" and designates those Christians who embraced the theological decisions put forth at the Council of Chalcedon in 451. The Melkites are the second largest Catholic community after the Maronites of Lebanon. They live mostly in Syria, Lebanon and Palestine (especially in the Galilee region), where they count some 400,000 members.

The final group of churches in the Catholic family are those formed out of the three Oriental Orthodox communions: Syrian, Coptic and Armenian. All maintain relationships and deep ties both to the Orthodox churches from which they came and to the Church of Rome.

The Syrian Catholic Church began in 1662. A century later, in 1774, the **Syrian Catholic Patriarchate of Antioch** was established. It remained in Eastern Turkey until political and religious upheavals required a relocation to Beirut in 1899. Ignatios Antoun II Hayek serves the church as its current patriarch. Some 35,000 members constitute this church today. They are dispersed in Syria, Iraq, Lebanon, Egypt and Jordan.

The **Coptic Catholic Patriarchate of Alexandria** traces its origin to the year 1824. The church now numbers approximately 100,000 members in Egypt. In both its modified Coptic liturgy and daily interaction, this community of faith retains a close tie with the large Coptic Orthodox Church from which it was born. The patriarch, Stephanos II, resides in Cairo.

The Armenian Catholics are the most recent members of this family of churches. Although some Armenian Orthodox converted to Catholicism as early as the fourteenth century, the **Armenian Catholic Patriarchate** was not established formally until 1840. For nearly one hundred years, the patriarch remained in Turkey. The tragedy of Armenian genocide earlier this century forced the church to relocate its headquarters to Beirut. Small Armenian Catholic communities live in various parts of the Middle East and the West, but the large majority of the 35,000 members are in Lebanon and Syria today.

4. The Evangelical (Protestant) Churches

The Protestant and Anglican churches, usually called Evangelical churches by Middle Easterners, make up the fourth family. These churches have sprung up in various places largely as a result of nineteenth- and twentieth-century missionary efforts by Western Protestant churches. Though often small, the number and diversity of congregations are large. Since we cannot adequately survey this complex scene, our focus will center on the larger denominations. These churches include most Middle Eastern Evangelicals. They are also the Protestant churches participating in the regional ecumenical movement defined by the Middle East Council of Churches.

A study of Protestant mission history reveals cooperative agreements whereby churches divided up the mission fields. These "comity" agreements were primarily arranged between churches in the U.S. The pattern is demonstrated in the Middle East: from the U.S., Presbyterians sent missionaries to Syria, Lebanon, Egypt and Iran; Anglicans to Palestine and Egypt; the Congregational Church (now part of the United Church of Christ) worked in Turkey; the Reformed Church went to the Arabian Gulf states; and the Methodists' mission focused on Arabic-speaking countries of North Africa.

Numerous other churches — for example, Southern Baptists, Quakers, Nazarenes, Assemblies of God — have had active mission histories that were not limited in geographical scope by comity arrangements. Most recently, especially in the past two decades, scores of missionaries from Western para-church organizations — such as World Vision, the Navigators, The "700 Club" and ministries of the Christian Broadcasting Network — have poured into the Middle East.

The response to Western missionaries sent by denominational agencies has been mixed. The same is true for the earlier Catholic mission efforts that produced the uniate churches. On the one hand, these missionary endeavors have contributed greatly in areas of education, health care and social services. On the other hand, many Orthodox Middle Easterners have not appreciated proselytizing efforts by some of the missionaries. In many cases, the failure to convert substantial numbers of Muslims — an ostensible purpose for being there — led Protestants to shift their energies to "converting" indigenous Christians. The phenomenon is known less-than-affectionately as "sheep stealing."

To Middle Eastern Christians this proselytizing makes it appear that many Evangelicals did not appreciate or even accept

the validity of their Christian faith. Some complain that the most
zealous missionaries act as though the Orthodox are not really
Christians or, perhaps, "not Christian enough." Consequently, the
relations between missionary agencies and personnel and Middle
Eastern churches have not always been harmonious. These dynamics have improved substantially in recent decades. Relationships with
the rapidly growing numbers of para-church organizations are a
distinctly different matter, one to which we will return later.

Some Protestant Communities   The largest Protestant community is found among the populous Egyptians. The Synod of the
Nile of the Evangelical Church of Egypt numbers more than 250,000
faithful. This church, which dates from the 1860s, became independent from the then United Presbyterian Church of North America
in 1957. The much smaller, but slightly older, National Synod of
Syria and Lebanon includes about 4,000 members. The Evangelical Church of Iran similarly began with Presbyterian missionaries.
By 1934, however, all the Protestants in Iran had united into one
independent national church.

The Anglican province in the region is called the Episcopal
Church of Jerusalem and the Middle East. It has two major centers: Jerusalem and Cyprus. The jurisdiction of the Episcopal Bishop
of Jerusalem, currently Samir Kafity, extends throughout Israel/
Palestine and Jordan. The diocese of Cyprus incorporates both the
island nation (where the British still maintain a substantial presence)
and the Gulf region. Smaller communities are served by the dioceses
of Egypt and Iran centered in Cairo and Tehran, respectively. This
configuration dates to a reorganization of Anglican jurisdictions in
1973.

Lutheran missionaries also came to the Holy Land in the nineteenth century, primarily from Europe. U.S. Lutherans (combined
today in the Evangelical Lutheran Church in America) have now
joined their work among Palestinians and Jordanians. Since 1958 this
church has been called the Evangelical Lutheran Church in Jordan.
Though small, it is one of the more visible communities since its
beautiful church building and bishopric are near the church of the
Holy Sepulcher in the old city of Jerusalem. Bishop Daud Haddad
presides over this community of faith.

In addition to the Orthodox and Assyrian Christians in the Gulf
region, the Reformed Church in America has had an active ministry
there for over a century. Because of the unique economic circum-

stances related to the oil industry, a primary focus for ministry in Kuwait, Bahrain, Iraq and Oman has been with expatriate workers. Before the 1991 war, hundreds of thousands of expatriate workers were resident in the Gulf. Because its ministry was already located here, the Reformed Church has been instrumental in facilitating relief efforts and in helping interpret events in the region during and after the crisis. The future shape of its ministry remains an open question in the uncertain aftermath of the devastating war.

The mission efforts of two other U.S. denominations involved in the comity arrangements also continue. The United Church of Christ's work in Turkey now concentrates primarily in the areas of secondary and university education, a major publishing house and social service ministry carried out through the Development Foundation of Turkey. In the North African countries of Tunisia and Algeria, United Methodist missionaries continue their witness by serving several local congregations in major cities.

5. *The Assyrian Church of the East*

The final category of Middle Eastern churches is the Assyrian Church of the East. Its singular history and minimal relationships with other Middle East Christian bodies preclude grouping this church in a family. Longstanding doctrinal disagreement and physical separation are still evident today. While there have been some efforts toward rapprochement, the Assyrians are the only indigenous church remaining outside the ecumenical relationships of the Middle East Council of Churches.

The church, which accepts the doctrine of the first two ecumenical councils, became a distinct body following the excommunication of its bishops — most notably Nestorius — at the decisive council in Ephesus in 431. Over the centuries the Assyrian Church has repeatedly endured persecution and dispersal as a result of its isolation. Its patriarchate has been moved many times. The official seat is in Baghdad, Iraq, today; the incumbent Catholicos, Patriarch Mar Denka IV, resides at the church headquarters in Chicago.

The Assyrian Church now includes about 250,000 members. The largest communities are in Iraq and North America, each counting some 80,000 adherents. Churches in Syria, Iran, India and Australia range from 30,000 to 15,000. Smaller groupings of churches are found in Lebanon and Western Europe.

CHANGING PATTERNS
OF INTERCHURCH RELATIONS

The churches in the Middle East, long separated by political and doctrinal differences, have moved steadily toward cooperative new relationships in the twentieth century. This movement has resulted both from internal dynamics within the churches and the larger, worldwide ecumenical movement.

Several major new streams have converged with the ancient, continuous rivers of faith to change the course of recent church history in the Middle East. One new stream flows from ecumenical cooperation in the Middle East. Throughout this century cooperative efforts among Western mission and service agencies have grown. In addition to these collaborative efforts among well-established church agencies, new initiatives were launched in the wake of the tumultuous upheavals in 1947–48 when Israel and Palestine were partitioned. The contemporary work of Church World Service and Witness (CWSW), the relief development and human service division of the National Council of Churches in the U.S.A., is rooted in these events.

The effort to meet emergency medical, housing and food needs of displaced Palestinian refugees was one of the first major overseas programs of this agency. The Canadian Council of Churches and various European church agencies joined these efforts a few years later as their ecumenical structures developed. The institutional framework for Western-based ecumenical relief and development work was provided initially by the Near East Christian Council (NECC), the predecessor of the Middle East Council of Churches (MECC).

The Worldwide Ecumenical Movement

Another stream flows from the worldwide ecumenical movement. The formative stages of the World Council of Churches (WCC) during the 1940s and 1950s were creative and experimental years for many churches, including those in the Middle East. The Orthodox churches participated in various ecumenical consultations. They also were related to agencies that merged into the WCC. The WCC was formed in 1948 by the coming together of several ecumenical organizations that had come into being to meet needs recognized by churches in many parts of the world during the twentieth century. These included the Universal Christian Council for Life and Work and the Faith and Order Movement. These two organizations intended to express the visible unity of the church and work on specific issues. The former concentrated on practical problems confronting the church in society; the latter dealt mostly with issues of doctrine and the constitution of the church.

Another major world organization, the International Missionary Council, joined the WCC formally in 1961 after years of cooperation. Many Middle Eastern churches had close links with the International Missionary Council throughout this century. In fact, the second of the Missionary Council's three great world assemblies was held in Jerusalem in 1928. (The first took place in Edinburgh in 1910 and the third in Tambaram, near Madras, in 1938.)*

The Eastern Orthodox Church, and subsequently the Oriental Orthodox churches, formally joined the WCC in the early 1960s. And, as we have noted above, several key Middle Eastern church officials have served the WCC in leadership positions during the past three decades. Most recently, at the WCC's Seventh World Assembly (1991) in Canberra, Australia, another Middle East church leader accepted a pivotal appointment. Bishop Aram Kishishian, the Armenian Orthodox bishop of Beirut, was selected to serve as the Moderator of the WCC's Central Committee until the next Assembly meets in 1998.

Orthodox-Catholic relations are still another tributary feeding ecumenical cooperation in the lands of the Bible. New, more hopeful relations between these communities, which together constitute 95 percent of the Middle Eastern Christian churches, developed during the 1950s and 1960s. Individually and collectively, the Middle Eastern churches have improved their relations with Rome steadily during the past three decades. In the early 1960s and thereafter, efforts to heal the deep divisions bore fruit during the Roman Catholic Vatican Council II. This pattern of growing mutuality in ministry was manifest in a dramatic new way in January 1990 at the MECC's Fifth General Assembly. At that historic meeting, the various Catholic churches in the Middle East, acting with the full blessing and support of Rome, joined the MECC as the fourth family of churches.

---

*Information about the ecumenical organizations that formed the WCC as well as about the MECC and the "families" of Middle Eastern churches can be found in the *Dictionary of the Ecumenical Movement*, edited by N. Lossky, J. Míguez Bonino, J. Pobee, T. Stransky, G. Wainwright and P. Webb (Geneva: WCC and Grand Rapids, Eerdmans, 1991).

Perhaps the most significant factor stimulating the Middle Eastern churches to ecumenism came from within. The 1940s witnessed the birth of a major renewal movement among Orthodox youth. Highly educated and deeply committed Orthodox youth in different churches discovered one another even as they brought new vitality to their respective communions. Many prominent leaders of this movement are now the leading bishops and patriarchs in the region and within the WCC. This invigorating renewal stimulated new relationships among the oldest churches at the same time that the larger ecumenical movement was establishing structures through which to channel their energies in cooperation with churches worldwide.

Institutional Relationships

During the 1960s and early 1970s, the communication and cooperation between Middle East churches and the NECC, the ecumenical body created by Protestant churches, continued to mature. Cooperative meetings and programs for theologians, educators, youth and church leaders were increasingly common. By 1974, the churches were poised to write a new chapter in their long history. In May of that year, representatives gathered in Nicosia, Cyprus, to create an indigenous ecumenical organization: The Middle East Council of Churches.

The MECC was constituted by three families of churches: Eastern Orthodox, Oriental Orthodox and Protestant. At its inaugural First General Assembly, the new organization identified its primary aims:

> To promote communion and ecumenical awareness among the churches in a manner by which each of them shall be able, through prayer, study and action, to participate in the riches of the tradition and spiritual experiences of the others; provide for means of common research with the view of understanding the traditions of the respective churches; broaden the field of cooperation between the churches with the purpose of carrying out the mission of the Church which is to proclaim the Gospel of Salvation; undertake and coordinate appropriate services for the expression of the common concern of the churches for all men and women; finally, to be a point of regional reference in the worldwide community of Christian churches, including relations with the World Council of Churches, regional and na-

tional councils of churches, all other churches of the region, and other ecumenical organizations.*

In the nearly two decades of its work, the MECC and its member churches have started and supported a wide range of programs related to education, women's issues, youth ministries and interfaith concerns. The guiding principles in these ongoing ministries have centered on strengthening Christian unity and the common witness of the churches. Spiritual renewal and solidarity are vital dimensions of the ecumenical movement as well, particularly in this volatile region where the minority Christian community often feels isolated and at the mercy of political developments occurring in the larger Muslim community.

Viewed from the perspective of two thousand years of church history, these contemporary developments are still in their infancy. Even so, the growth and changes indicate a substantial transformation is under way. But it is a transformation taking place amid extraordinarily trying circumstances. Wars and political upheavals have been a constant reality in the Middle East throughout most of the twentieth century. As a result, Middle East Christians have affirmed the necessity of pursuing stability and security for the people in the region, people who long for peace and justice.

The impact of major political crises and wars — from the Arab/Israeli wars of 1967 and 1973 to the civil war in Lebanon and the Iranian revolution — on Middle Eastern Christians was felt keenly by Western churches in partnership with them. These complex events underscored just how important it is for Christians in the Middle East and West to work together on policies to guide their many-sided relationships and ministries and to discuss where further work is required. The emerging ecumenical relationships we have mentioned provided one setting for this to happen. Individual churches, particularly those already in partnership with the Western Protestant denominations, represented another important setting for dialogue and work together.

Consider the complexity of ecumenical relationships churches in the Middle East may sustain. As desirable as the various relationships are, they can also create pressures for a church. The Evangelical Church in Egypt, for instance, has been closely related

---

*Information about MECC resources available in English may be obtained through many denominational and ecumenical offices or by writing to the MECC, Box 5378, Limassol, Cyprus.

to the Presbyterians in the U.S. Together they developed educational ministries and social service programs and built churches. The
ongoing relationship is greatly valued. At the same time, Egyptian
Evangelicals are an independent church, and they feel themselves
to be part of the predominantly Orthodox Christian community in
Egypt. At times, the need for close cooperation and strong unity
within Egypt has been especially crucial, particularly when revivalist
Islamic movements have sought to exercise political power in ways
threatening to the Christian minority.

When we widen the circle a bit more, we see the Egyptian Evangelicals in relationship with other Protestants in the context of the
NECC and, subsequently, the larger community of Christians gathered in the MECC. How can they define themselves with integrity
and, at the same time, participate creatively with partner churches in
the West and other churches in the Middle East? Answers can sel-
dom be clear-cut in a setting where several patterns of relationships
shift from time to time.

In a focused effort to help clarify relationships and mutual responsibilities, the National Council of Churches in the U.S.A. took
the lead in developing a new policy base for U.S. churches in 1978.
A painstaking two-and-one-half year process led to the adoption of
the "NCC Middle East Policy Statement" by the NCC Governing
Board in 1980. A blue-ribbon panel traveled to the region and consulted widely with Middle Eastern people as well as with North
American Christians, Jews and Muslims. Various draft documents
were debated and refined in an effort to address the deeply felt
concerns of all people and groups drawn into Middle East events.
The document expresses well the churches' basis for ecumenical
ministries and provides a framework for the future. A brief excerpt
conveys the new spirit of cooperation:

> Among the member churches of the Middle East Council of
> Churches and the National Council of the Churches of Christ
> in the U.S.A., this is a relationship of partners who are called
> to express their unity in Christ. The relationship presumes
> the equality of partners in every respect and evokes a spirit
> of mutuality among these various members of the Body of
> Christ. Given this basic understanding, a chief responsibility of
> the National Council of the Churches of Christ in the U.S.A.
> is to nurture a variety of relationships, formal and informal,
> designed to foster unity and mutual understanding between
> U.S.A. and Middle East churches. The geographical consider-

ations that informed past mission comity agreements of the
Protestant and Anglican churches, while a sign of western
Christian cooperation in their time, are no longer appropriate since Middle East evangelical churches have developed
their own autonomy and relationships. Future relationships
should give evidence of unity and mutual respect among the
churches.*

The NCC policy statement goes on to identify specific guidelines
and tasks for its 32 U.S. member churches. In addition, the document provides guidelines in two other major areas: relations with
people of other faiths and the witness of the churches in society. We
will look more closely at those opportunities and responsibilities in
chapters 3 and 4. But first we turn to consider some ways that many
churches in the U.S. and Canada and churches in the Middle East
have sought to practice new models of mutuality in ministry.

---

*NCC "Middle East Policy Statement" (November 1980), p. 3. The policy state-
ment is available from the NCC Middle East Office, 475 Riverside Drive, #614,
New York, NY 10115, for a $1 printing and postage fee.

MINISTRIES OF WITNESS AND SERVICE

The Middle East Council of Churches (MECC) and its member churches carry out a variety of ministries, many in partnership with churches from Europe and North America. Education is a primary focus of their work. The churches are involved in education at all levels — from pre-school programs to graduate theological seminaries. They also work cooperatively at times to prepare curricula for church education, audiovisual projects and the like. In addition, the MECC oversees the operation of the Family Bookshops, a major bookstore chain operating in most Middle Eastern countries.

Medical care is another area of churches' mission. Working in conjunction with Western churches, Middle Eastern Christians staff and operate various hospitals and clinics throughout the region. Medical and educational institutions are among the most positive legacies of nineteenth- and twentieth-century missionary endeavors. In an area with many medical needs, these ministries by the minority Christian community are a powerful form of witness in the larger society.

The MECC also coordinates numerous programs among youth. Leadership training workshops, service projects and youth camps nurture young Christians and prepare them to lead the churches in the future. At the same time, the next generation of Christians is strengthening ties between churches in the homeland of Christianity.

Ecumenical programs on women's concerns also address current issues and look toward the future. The challenges posed by traditional male-dominated culture in the Middle East present a range of issues for the churches. The role of women in church leadership, for instance, challenges traditional patterns of relationships and structures. But the MECC seeks constructive ways for its churches to explore women's issues. Many women serve in key staff positions within the MECC. Increasingly, churches are appointing women as their representatives to ecumenical committees. In this area, partnership and mutuality within the larger ecumenical community should prove especially helpful because most churches are now wrestling with how best to fashion new, less restrictive frameworks for women and men working both in the churches and society at large.

Christian service ministries are the most extensive ecumenical efforts among Middle Eastern Christians today. The various ministries are rooted in biblical mandates concerning Christian behavior in the world: "You shall love your neighbor as yourself" (Matt. 22:39) and "In everything do to others as you would have them do to you; for this is the law and the prophets" (Matt. 7:12). Living as minority communities in predominantly Muslim — or, in the case of Israel, Jewish — societies, Middle Eastern Christians highlight how important responsible, self-giving service is as primary form of witness. In their service ministries, often called diaconal ministries, Christians both help meet pressing human needs and bear witness to the meaning of God's reconciling love made known through Jesus, the Christ.

Serving Neighbors

Some Western Christians, with their emphasis on verbal proclamation and evangelization as the singular means of "witness," appear to downplay such service ministries. But in many Middle Eastern countries (e.g., Egypt, Israel, Saudi Arabia) it is illegal to proselytize. Christians cannot overtly seek to convert Muslims or Jews, although many do continue to bear witness through preaching, teaching, distribution of Bibles and the like. In such restricted settings, particularly where poverty and war are ever-present realities, many Middle Eastern Christians cite the strong words of Jesus when he spoke of the coming judgment of the nations:

> When the Son of Man comes in his glory, and all the angels with him, then he will sit on the throne of his glory. All the nations will be gathered before him, and he will separate people one from another as a shepherd separates the sheep from the goats.... The righteous will answer him, "Lord, when was it that we saw you hungry and gave you food, or thirsty and gave you something to drink? And when was it that we saw you a stranger and welcomed you, or naked and gave you clothing? And when was it that we saw you sick or in prison and visited you?" And the king will answer them, "Truly I tell you, just as you did it to one of the least of these who are members of my family, you did it to me." (Matt. 25:31–32; 37–40)

The MECC and its member churches consciously endeavor to live out this mandate in tangible ways. And a growing number of North American communions are channeling their energies and resources ecumenically in support of such ministries. Working in partnership with the churches of the Middle East reaffirms that these churches are the primary manifestation of the body of Christ in this part of the world.

As churches have practiced partnership in mission, another truth has emerged: Western churches not only have resources and personnel to share, they also have much to learn and receive from their sisters and brothers in the Middle East. The ministries that witness through service demonstrate this truth. Christians living for centuries in the midst of political conflict and religious diversity have much to teach all of us who now live in a global community characterized by political conflict and religious diversity. Three examples of diaconal ministries carried out through the "Life and Service" program of the MECC illustrate the point.

Palestinian Refugees   For more than forty years, Middle Eastern and Western churches have worked among the Palestinian refugees. Initial efforts in the wake of the fighting and displacement of people in 1947 and 1948 focused on emergency needs: food, clothing, temporary housing and medical treatment. As the refugee status of Palestinians became more permanent, the programs adapted to help meet the needs. Today, the MECC's Department on Service to Palestinian Refugees carries on this work through a variety of ministries with the hundreds of thousands of Palestinians living in Gaza, the West Bank, Jordan, Lebanon and within the pre-1967 borders of Israel. The programs are coordinated and run by the MECC with assistance from Western churches and agencies. They include educational opportunities, health care, vocational training, small business loans and social service centers. One has only to visit a mother/baby clinic or vocational training center for carpentry in a refugee camp in Gaza to appreciate the value of such programs.

The powerful witness of such services should not be understated. While the social service ministries are carried out through the MECC structures, they are designed to benefit all Palestinians in need, without reference to religious persuasion. In the case of Gaza, for example, Muslims constitute 98 percent of the Palestinian community. The percentage of Christians among the Palestinian population in general is considerably higher, roughly 8 to 10 percent.

The ERRR   In Lebanon, the MECC conducts a large program for emergency relief, reconstruction and rehabilitation (ERRR). The program, based in West Beirut, is known throughout the country for its uniqueness. Unlike most other human service programs implemented

In Gaza, service projects are coordinated on behalf of many churches by the Middle East Council of Churches' Department on Service to Palestinian Refugees. Young women learn office skills in a business education class (right) and mothers and children wait to see a doctor at a family service center clinic (below). (Photos by David Weaver.)

since war broke out in 1975, the MECC seeks to assist people in need without discrimination. In the fragmented society enduring a multisided civil conflict, such a nonpartisan approach is especially crucial. It communicates across the various dividing lines that the people of Lebanon are in need, are interdependent and, with effort, can reach out to others in a spirit of cooperation and peace.

The ERRR program has faced numerous challenges through the intense fighting and lulls in the Lebanese conflict. Partner churches in Europe and North America have consistently supported the MECC's efforts to meet various emergency needs, assist in reconstruction, land reclamation, and so on. For more than a decade, North American churches have provided between $400,000 and $1 million annually in funds, medicine, tents, blankets, and other supplies. In many instances, the churches have found specialized personnel to assist with particular tasks for a set period. In 1986, for example, the Canadian Council of Churches seconded two people to the MECC for work in Lebanon: Sandra Ballentyne, to serve as a physical therapist, and Douglas du Charme, to help coordinate overall relief efforts and teach part-time in the Near East School of Theology. After these tasks were successfully completed during two years of service, the MECC reassessed its needs. In response to the MECC's request, du Charme was reappointed to work with the staff of the MECC's General Secretariat on a range of projects.

Response to the Gulf War Crisis   A third example of diaconal ministry occurred in the 1990–91 Gulf crisis. In the immediate wake of the Iraqi invasion of Kuwait, hundreds of thousands of foreign workers lost their jobs and were forced to flee the fighting. Within days, a major human tragedy began to unfold as these people fled toward Jordan, leaving behind most possessions. Only a fraction of the refugees were able to cross into Jordan. The large majority — from Pakistan, Sri Lanka, the Philippines, Palestine and elsewhere — were trapped on the Jordanian-Iraqi border with no provisions. Most nations, preoccupied with events in Kuwait, did little to assist these hapless people. Their plight worsened daily.

The MECC was among the first on the scene. The experience of working in crisis situations and the commitment to assist all people in need proved invaluable. Working with the governments involved and with the supportive resources of concerned Christians worldwide, the MECC staff organized the emergency relief work among the different agencies on the scene.

In North America, events emerge and fade quickly in the news; media attention shifts to new, breaking stories. The human needs created by the Gulf crisis have not ceased simply because the cameras were turned off; rather, they have grown in the months after the fighting ceased. Several million people affected directly by the crisis still face long-term consequences. These include the more than 2.5 million expatriate workers who fled Iraq and Kuwait, Iraqi and Kuwaiti civilians, Kurdish refugees in the north of Iraq and Iraqi Shi'ites in the south. The MECC's "Life and Service" work continues to focus resources and energies on the needs of these people, whether or not the Western media acknowledges the human tragedy.

Partnership in Ministry

Churches in the West are privileged to participate in support of the MECC's service ministries. In this way, Christians are actively providing for the needs of people; they are helping develop and maintain vital social infrastructures (particularly where governments are not doing so); they are also helping the local Christian communities to help themselves and others through cooperative projects that, in the end, foster respect and understanding. In the process, Western Christians can deepen their understanding of responsible service and witness as well as of interreligious cooperation. These are valuable lessons for all of us who seek to live peacefully in our fragile global village.

Middle Eastern churches provide financial support and staff; external funds are also needed. Many churches in the U.S. and Canada provide resources to the MECC through the ecumenical channels of the NCC and the Canadian Council of Churches. Some designate funds from such special offerings as the "One Great Hour of Sharing" for ecumenical relief work. Others contribute a portion of funds given for the human service ministries carried out by their denominations. In Canada, the churches often work with their government to secure resources for social service ministries like the Department on Service to Palestinian Refugees and the ERRR. And in the U.S., hundreds of thousands of individuals contribute directly to the ecumenical ministries of Church World Service and Witness through hundreds of CROP walks in communities all across the land. Seventy-five percent of the funds raised by CWSW/CROP is used for national and international human service ministries; 25 percent stays in local communities for their human service needs.*

Many Christians in the West are not aware fully of the ways they and their churches are already working in partnership with the MECC and individual churches in the region. Although much more needs to be done to strengthen such ministries, it is important for North Americans to recognize how much their churches and ecumenical agencies are doing. Their support of denominational programs and CROP walks help make possible the vital ministries of Christians like those of the churches in the Middle East.

Social service ministries by local Christians have benefits beyond actual help to people in need. They also present a positive message of reconciliation, interdependence and hope. The need for this kind of witness in the Middle East is especially urgent when compared to activities of many Western-based Christian groups and para-church organizations.

---

*CROP is the acronym for Christian Rural Overseas Program. Although the CROP program is now lodged within the NCC's division of Church World Service and Witness, the name is still used as CWSW/CROP in many settings.

THE IMPACT OF PARA-CHURCH GROUPS

Today more than forty Western-based para-church organizations are conducting Middle East programs. These organizations are Christian in orientation and theology, but are not based in a recognized denominational body. Many of these groups pursue programs designed to help people in need. While they undoubtedly accomplish some good, the para-church groups often create serious problems as well. Virtually all of these organizations are operated by theologically conservative or fundamentalist Christians. As such, they tend to be distant from ecumenical perspectives and structures. They frequently come to the region to work without reference to the concerns of the large majority of Middle Eastern churches. And they bring with them a great deal of theological and political baggage.

The Christian Broadcasting Network (CBN) of Pat Robertson, for instance, runs a television ministry in southern Lebanon. Its theological approach identifies the contemporary state of Israel as the critical piece in the unfolding biblical drama. As a result, it tends toward uncritical support for the policies — political and military — pursued by whatever Israeli government is in power. It doesn't take an advanced degree in political science to perceive ways in which Western Christians, extolling the virtue of Israeli policies to the people of southern Lebanon over the television airwaves, will create difficulties. At the very least, such programs emphasize, or sometimes create, barriers between the Christians and Muslims living in Lebanon.

Caught in a multisided civil war made worse by a history of regional and superpower intervention, Lebanon's various communities find their fears and anxieties heightened by such heavy-handed political rhetoric. Many local Christians, who have lived side by side with Muslim neighbors for centuries, are now being perceived as a threat to Muslims. Some, particularly among the extremist Muslim factions, simplistically associate all Christians with the evangelical/fundamentalist Western Christians with high media visibility. A growing number of Muslims are viewing their local Christian neighbors in Lebanon as somehow an alien presence and a potential threat to their aspirations.

Intense interest in the contemporary Middle East is a common feature of many para-church organizations and television ministries. This theological fervor was manifest during the 1991 Gulf war. On religious broadcasting stations, program after program featured "expert" Bible scholars discussing the signs of the impending Armageddon. These "experts" confidently pieced together the puzzle of their theological plan for "the end times." Most also peddled books, cassette tapes and videos. Judging by bestseller lists and radio talk shows, several million North American Christians were caught up in the effort to decipher the "signs" surrounding events in the Gulf crisis to determine if the final showdown at Armageddon was at hand.

Making Prophecies Fit

One result of such theological fixations is that the people who are living through the events in question are dehumanized. They become objects of the theological scheme. I saw this dynamic several years ago during a lengthy conversation at the "Christian Embassy" in Jerusalem. A colleague and I spent almost two hours in conversation with one of the top officials of this para-church organization whose stated aim was to "comfort the people of Israel." Toward the end of our discussion — which felt more like a monologue aimed at prospective supporters of their work — my colleague mentioned concern for recent violence involving Israelis and Palestinians in Lebanon. He said he was distressed over the pain and suffering experienced by people on both sides of the conflict. Without hesitation the official responded: "These recent events are all part of God's unfolding plan. The Jews don't even understand what God is doing! But we do. It is an exciting time to be here and watch God shaping events for the second coming of Christ." The very people this man claimed to be there to "comfort" were, in the last analysis, not much more than the object of his theology.

Another feature of the approach most U.S. para-church groups take toward the Middle East is their political ideology. During the Gulf war, religious broadcasts often featured the host or preacher poised in front of a gigantic flag. Having watched many hours of such broadcasts, I was struck by how few offered anything but uncritical support for all U.S. policy decisions. The line between church and state, cherished in theory, was not easy to discern. In an era of satellite communications, such images are viewed around the world. Imagine what impression such a combination makes on Christians, Muslims and Jews living in the Middle East.

In spite of these features, some churches in the Middle East do accept financial assistance from para-church groups. Their needs

are often overwhelming and resources scarce. And some have suggested that by working with the Western evangelical organizations —
both para-church organizations and denominational bodies unfamiliar with ecumenism — it may be possible to help them understand
the perspectives and concerns of Middle Eastern Christians. To a
certain extent, this is happening.

Cautious Collaboration

Since 1985, an informal coalition of U.S.-based evangelical and para-
church leaders have been meeting with staff from the MECC and
a few evangelical Christians working on Middle East issues within
church structures. The group, known as "Evangelicals for Middle
East Understanding," has met in Richmond, Washington and Atlanta.
In the fall of 1991, over fifty people in this group traveled to Cyprus
and various parts of the Middle East for a two-week educational
opportunity hosted by the MECC.

The message from Middle Eastern Christians to these evangelical leaders is the same as the message they convey consistently
to ecumenically oriented Christians and churches. In summary, the
message goes something like this:

> The Christians in the Middle East both need and appreciate the
> material assistance provided by North American Christians. It is
> crucial for their ongoing ministries in the midst of political and
> religious upheaval. However, the primary problems they face
> lie in the political arena. The overriding concern is for durable
> peace and stability in their societies. If peace with justice can be
> achieved, many other societal problems will become less severe.
> More than anything else, Christians in the Middle East want
> North Americans to become well informed about the Middle
> East and then to encourage their own governments to work
> strenuously for a just and durable peace.

People of faith and goodwill cannot ignore the implications of
this challenge: partnership with our sisters and brothers in the
Middle East requires education and advocacy here in North America. Accordingly, we turn next to consider major political dynamics
influencing events in the Middle East today.

3

Untangling
the Political Web

THE CAUSES OF CONFLICT

Historically, religious bodies...have accepted (even asserted) responsibility for initiating and sustaining moral discourse on public issues of justice and political responsibility.... The religious community as such possesses an angle of vision which is different from that of the political party, the university or the research institute.

Specifically, the Christian community understands itself to be a community of conscience. Belief in a just and loving God is expected to have consequences in human relationships. The complexity of events, the sinful nature of persons and society, and human fears make it difficult to bring an informed conscience to bear on issues of policy; the more difficult, the more necessary.*

These words identify a major element of Christian responsibility in the face of conflict, injustice and war in the Middle East. We are to be a community of conscience. Concerted efforts by individuals and religious groups can help raise the level of informed discussion within society. We are also to help create a climate in which

_____
*NCC "Middle East Policy Statement," p. 6.

government leaders are more likely to pursue a just peace than a just war.

Responsible citizenship and a ministry of reconciliation require effort. Peacemaking begins with education. Without question, today's Middle East situation includes many, often complex issues. But they are not beyond comprehension. It is possible — indeed, necessary — to begin developing a coherent frame of reference. One need not become a Middle East expert to reflect thoughtfully and make informed judgments. The basic question is this: Do we care enough to invest the time and energy necessary to develop a framework for understanding? In view of the various ways North American Christians are already linked with people and events in the Middle East, the answer clearly should be yes.

Turbulent developments in the Middle East have become standard fare on the nightly news. The coverage elicits a response. It is important to recognize that our response or even the way we frame our questions reveals our assumptions and shapes our conclusions. To illustrate, consider one reaction that many people offer to virtually all conflict situations in the Middle East: "There will never be peace in the Middle East. Those people have been fighting each other for thousands of years." Not only are such comments erroneous, but they imply that Middle Eastern people are inherently violent. And, if you presuppose that "those people" are always going to fight, you also presuppose that there is nothing we (presumably the more "civilized" people) can do to help. In effect, this response serves to absolve "us" from any responsibility.

It makes all the difference if we begin with other assumptions, namely: people in the Middle East are human beings who live, laugh and love; people in the Middle East cry, feel pain and experience loss; people in the Middle East desire peace, security, economic well-being and a better future for their children. In short, the lives of people in Middle East are affected by various circumstances just like the lives of people everywhere else. Obviously, the dynamics at work in many parts of the Middle East are considerably more unpredictable than are those in, say, Sweden or Switzerland.

With less narrow presuppositions, we can frame our questions to leave open the search for answers: What is going on here? Why is there so much widespread instability and unrest? What is motivating various people and groups? Why do governments behave as they do?

The answers are not always straightforward. Frequently, there are several factors at work, several sources of unrest contributing to a particular situation. We cannot here probe deeply specific issues and politics in Jordan, Syria, Iran, Egypt, Cyprus and so on. We must both cast our net more broadly and, at the same time, remain modest about the limits of our focus in this study. But we can begin to untangle the political web when we understand the major roots of discontent and frustration present in the region.

Our approach in this section focuses on major issues confronting people throughout the region: the rights of minorities, protection of human rights, self-determination, clarifying nation-state boundaries, economic disparity, the need for security and the arms race. These unresolved issues, rooted in the twentieth-century history of the Middle East, contribute to instability and unrest. Understanding this history helps make sense of the more visible events that capture headlines in the international media. Several of these issues were prominent during the 1990–91 Gulf crisis. And most of the major regional concerns are factors in the Israeli-Palestinian dispute, the most far-reaching regional conflict.

Our survey helps us in two ways. First, by clarifying elements that stimulate and feed conflict, we can begin to understand the Middle East more accurately. Second, understanding major sources of unrest better equips us to encourage constructive policies by our government leaders. We can more readily identify principled positions that, if applied consistently, will address the sources of conflict, not simply the symptoms.

Roots of Instability*

As we have noted in chapter 1, the region continues to live with complications stemming from a long history of foreign domination. The roots run deep into both Ottoman and colonial rule. The process of transition from Ottoman to European domination occurred in the course of two centuries as the Ottomans yielded territory to European powers. After World War I, the Treaty of Versailles recognized that the Arab lands previously under Ottoman rule should become independent under the guidance of the nations given the "mandate" for them. The League of Nations formally granted this "mandate" to the British and French governments in 1922. The specific areas were Palestine and Iraq for the British; Syria and Lebanon for the

---

*This section is an expanded version of material first published by Charles A. Kimball in "The Case for Diplomacy: Settling Regional Disputes in an Interdependent World," *Sojourners* (February–March 1991): 18–21.

French. In addition, the British were the dominant power in Egypt, Cyprus, Oman, Bahrain and several other areas that would become Gulf states. The French colonial empire also extended across a large portion of Arabic-speaking North Africa (called the Maghreb).

The motives that shaped British and French policy decisions during the 1920s, 1930s and 1940s were predictably self-serving. The renowned Middle East scholar Albert Hourani summarizes European sovereignty in his superb study, *A History of the Arab Peoples*:

> Firmly placed in their positions of power, Britain and France were able in the period 1918–39 to expand their control over the trade and production of the region. The Arab world was still primarily important for Europe as a source of raw materials.... There were also more extended interests: Britain's presence in the Middle East helped maintain her position as a Mediterranean power and a world power. The sea-route to India and the Far East ran through the Suez Canal. Air-routes across the Middle East were also being developed in the 1920s and 1930s.*

Some aspects of colonial influence were positive for the inhabitants. Considerable capital investments helped improve the roads, railroads, irrigation and cultivation systems. Oil resources in the Gulf, cotton in Egypt, and mineral resources in various countries were developed and now represent major industries. In addition, educational opportunities increased substantially for segments of the local population. This legacy lives on today in Syria and Lebanon, for instance, where a large percentage of leaders still speak French as well as Arabic. Many universities and secondary schools in Syria, Lebanon, Palestine and elsewhere were established by Western missionaries. In some settings, such as among the Maronite Christians in Lebanon, local Christians benefited from these educational opportunities far more than the society at large.

A Patchwork Legacy: Iraq   While most Middle Easterners will acknowledge some positive benefits from the era of European colonial domination, they more readily cite the problems and negative consequences flowing from this history. In fact, many of the current problems in the region relate directly to policy decisions of ruling European powers. One prominent example is the current configuration

---

*Albert Hourani, *A History of the Arab Peoples* (Cambridge, Mass.: Harvard University Press, 1991), pp. 320–21.

of national borders. In the processes leading toward independence, new and frequently artificial boundaries were drawn. The problematic nature of the boundaries related to Iraq and Kuwait and to Israel/Palestine has been a central feature in their conflicts.

Soon after Saddam Hussein's forces invaded Kuwait, he declared that Kuwait was the "nineteenth province" of Iraq. Hussein stressed that Kuwait was a creation of the British colonialists. In one sense he was correct. Kuwait did not exist as a sovereign state before 1962. Kuwait's twentieth-century history is very much bound up with British colonial interests, most notably the massive oil reserves under these lands. What Saddam Hussein did not stress in his public statements, however, was the similarly artificial nature of Iraq itself.

Iraq today is a patchwork of five Ottoman provinces. The decisions leading to the formation of Iraq created problems for people directly affected. Consider the case of the Kurds. After promising the Kurds a homeland, the colonial authorities decided instead simply to divide them between Iraq, Turkey, Iran and Syria. As a result, the Kurds have suffered as minority communities in each of these settings. The Kurds have a strong religious, cultural and linguistic heritage. But some countries will not allow them to teach their language to their children in school. Their deep frustration with Saddam Hussein in Iraq has led to popular revolts, most recently in the aftermath of the Gulf war. The colonial borders fail to take seriously the natural grouping of these people. Until this issue is addressed equitably, the Kurds will continue to resist the governments with authority over them.

Without a Homeland: Armenians and Palestinians   Two other groups with strong national identities have also been left out of the nation-state configuration: Armenians and Palestinians. The Armenians are dispersed throughout the area — indeed, throughout the world. Still, they maintain a strong sense of group/national identity. Having suffered the horror of genocide earlier this century in Turkey, they deeply desire a more secure future. In view of their history, they are understandably nervous because they live as small, politically powerless communities in most areas. There is, perhaps, reason for hope in the 1990s. Soviet Armenia is one of the republics that declared independence from the U.S.S.R. in September 1991.

The Armenians will continue to be a minority community in Lebanon, Syria, Iraq and elsewhere. Their hope mirrors that of most Christians living in predominantly Islamic countries (or the predominantly Jewish state of Israel): to live in peaceful co-existence in societies that assure full freedom to worship and exercise political rights without discrimination.

Like the Kurds, the Palestinian Arabs were promised a homeland earlier this century. The British authorities also made promises to assist in establishing a Jewish national home in Palestine. The seemingly incompatible promises made to these two peoples for the same land created expectations and fueled frustrations over the decades. In addition, British policies fluctuated with changing governments and shifting priorities. By the time the British "mandate" ended and the new states were to be established, the issues were far from resolved. United Nations Resolution 181, adopted on November 29, 1947, called for a partition of Palestine into a Jewish Israeli and a Palestinian Arab state. The Israelis accepted the plan; the Arabs did not. The war that ensued in 1948 resulted in Israeli control of an even larger portion of the area; tens of thousands of Palestinian Arabs became refugees. The conflict has continued to plague the people in the region for more than four decades.

Unrepresentative Governments, Unpopular Policies

Another legacy of the colonial era is the unrepresentative governments in the Middle East. As the new nation-states were formed, local leaders were installed by European powers. Kings and ruling families were established in Jordan, Iraq and Kuwait, for instance. The dynasties continue in Jordan with King Hussein and in Kuwait with the Emir as the head of the Al-Sabah family. In Iraq, a succession of military-led coups toppled the monarch and resulted finally in the government led by Saddam Hussein's Baathist Party.

In 1992, most Middle Eastern countries are ruled by autocratic governments. Rarely are these governments in power by virtue of popular choice. Generals and kings may be home-grown, but that does not make them representative of their people. In fact, many of the current leaders in the Middle East are notorious for their repressive policies. The lack of democracy and the denial of many basic human rights is all too common in the region. Human rights reports on Middle Eastern governments by groups such as Amnesty International, Middle East Watch — even the U.S. Department of State — make grim reading. We hasten to add that appalling human rights records and repressive policies are not unique to the Middle East. The same dreadful practices are hauntingly familiar in many Latin

HUMAN RIGHTS REPORT

Each year the U.S. Department of State prepares a country-by-country human rights report for public distribution. The following brief excerpts come from the 1990 report under sections titled "Torture and Other Cruel, Inhuman, or Degrading Treatment or Punishment."

TURKEY

While the Turkish Constitution outlaws torture, and Turkey is a signatory to several international conventions proscribing it, pervasive and credible reports of torture persist throughout Turkey.... Knowledgeable observers contend that many persons charged with political crimes are tortured and that significant numbers charged with ordinary crimes are subjected to police brutality.... Credible reports indicate that systematic beatings, including beatings on the soles of the feet, high-pressure cold water hoses, electric shocks, and hanging by the arms are methods commonly employed. Psychological abuse in the form of verbal intimidation and threats is also said to be common. Interviews with former detainees tend to confirm that these types of abuse occur. Several former detainees gave similar descriptions of a torture facility and the methods employed by the police at the "Deep Investigation Laboratory" (DAL) in Ankara. (p. 1287)

ISRAEL AND THE OCCUPIED TERRITORIES

Reports continue of harsh and demeaning treatment of prisoners under investigation of interrogation, as well as beatings of suspects. Critics state that prisoner mistreatment takes the form of slaps and blows and similar practices, including enforced standing in one position for prolonged periods, hooding, sleep deprivation, cold showers, and incarceration in unclean and physically confining spaces. These practices reportedly have continued since they were confirmed in the 1987 report of the officially appointed Landau Commission.... Most convictions in security cases are based on confessions. An attorney is normally not allowed to see a client until after interrogation is completed and a confession, if obtained, has been made.... Physical and psychological pressures, and reduced sentences for those who confess, contribute to the likelihood that security detainees will sign confessions. Confessions are usually recorded in Hebrew, which many defendants are unable to read. (pp. 1479–84)

American, African and Asian countries and lie close beneath the surface of our own societies.

We also need to be aware that independent states are often far from independent. Particular policy decisions in a given country are rarely made in isolation. A variety of relationships bind the different countries to others in the region as well as to the larger global powers. The intricate web of regional and global political interaction often creates a dynamic of dependency. Individual countries may be heavily dependent or burdened by such realities as shifting political alliances, the perceived need for military and economic aid, and foreign debt. When we look at a given country, these dynamics come into sharp relief.

Jordan   Recall the case of Jordan during the Gulf crisis. From the beginning of the crisis in August 1990, Jordan was in a no-win position. On the one hand, King Hussein had managed for decades to nurture close relations with the U.S., Saudi Arabia and others who aligned against Iraq. At the same time, Jordan's economy depended heavily on relations with neighboring Iraq. Add another complicating factor: the large majority of people living in Jordan are Palestinians. Not surprisingly, the popular political sentiment in Jordan favored Saddam Hussein, because his rhetoric clearly supported Palestinian aspirations.

Jordan is an independent country. In the context of the Gulf crisis, however, all its political positions were shaped by interlocking internal and external relationships. When King Hussein publicly sided with Iraq, his country paid a high price: the U.S. and Saudi governments immediately suspended all aid to Jordan. Conversely, Egypt was heavily rewarded for its unequivocal support for policies of the U.S.-led allied coalition. Within days of Egypt's vote in the United Nations supporting the sanctions and later military actions against Iraq, the U.S. government announced that it was forgiving $8 billion of Egypt's foreign debt. Whatever the immediate consequences of such rewards and punishments, the resulting dependence and lack of control produce frustration both for governments and people.

In many settings the repressive policies of an unrepresentative government fuel popular discontent. In such cases, the option of protesting against one's own government may not be viable. In many instances, however, it is politically possible to vent frustration toward those external powers believed to be dominating one's own country. Thus, in the Middle East it is very common to find political

protests aimed at the U.S. and Israel. Their policies are perceived —
sometimes rightly, sometimes quite unfairly — as controlling or
manipulating events from outside.

Conflicting Visions

Another source of instability also relates to internal dissatisfaction
with ruling governments. Many people in the Middle East agree that
the status quo in their particular country is untenable. But there is
considerable disagreement on how best to structure a new society.

Islamic reform movements offer one type of vision or plan for
the future in most Middle Eastern countries today. The character
and methods of these various reform groups differ from place to
place. The Western media stereotype of extremist fanaticism associated with Islamic "fundamentalism" can be highly misleading. While
some religiously inspired groups with political agendas have employed violent tactics, most do not. The various Islamic movements
are united generally in the conviction that Islam can provide a viable
political, social and cultural model for ordering their societies.

Many Middle Easterners are disillusioned and annoyed with the
models of Western capitalism and Soviet socialism (now discredited
by its own people). Dissatisfaction with these models coupled with
a deep sense of pride in the glorious centuries of Islamic history
provide a basis for advocating the hope that Islam can provide an alternative way. Although few groups agree on what exactly an Islamic
state should look like or how it should function, a growing number
of people are persuaded that an Islamic state model represents the
way forward.

Many other Middle Easterners — Muslims, Christians and some
Jews — see major problems with nation-states defined along religious
lines. They argue that any "Islamic," "Jewish" or "Christian" state
will inevitably produce first-, second- and even third-class citizens.
They point to the ways discrimination becomes actualized toward Israeli Arabs and Iranian Bahais, for example. Thus, many who oppose
political reform along religious lines propose instead secular governments with structures in which the political and religious rights of
all groups are guaranteed.

The tensions present between and among people defining and
working toward alternative visions for their societies are real and
destabilizing. At times these tensions erupt into open confrontation.
To understand these visions and the tensions they produce accu-

rately, one must look at each country separately. Competing visions are advocated in Algeria, Egypt, Jordan, Iraq, Lebanon and elsewhere, but the specifics and nuances vary. Accurate understanding requires analysis of the separate settings. Casually lumping various Middle Eastern countries together for collective analysis makes no more sense than does grouping England, France, The Netherlands and Greece. These countries share a history in Western Europe and are populated predominantly by Christians. Even so, we know that the particular histories and current political realities in each country require that it be examined in its context. The same is true for states in the Middle East.

Disparity Between Rich and Poor

Another major source of frustration is the gross inequity in wealth and resources. The astonishing oil wealth controlled by Kuwait's ruling family, for instance, stands in stark contrast to the unspeakable poverty of Palestinian refugees in Gaza. During the war to liberate their country, the Kuwaiti government in exile pledged $13 billion to the U.S. for military expenses. This figure represented approximately the interest earnings for one year on the estimated $100 billion Kuwait has on deposit in foreign banks.

On many occasions I have led groups on study tours through the Middle East. Unlike most group travel itineraries in the Holy Land ours includes a day or two in Gaza. It is not what one would consider a day of fun and sun at the beach; it is, however, a significant learning experience. In every instance, the tour participants cite Gaza as one of the most moving and traumatic experiences for Western visitors. In 1988, after returning to Jerusalem, our group was meeting to talk about what we had seen and heard in Gaza. One CWSW/CROP staff person summed up the experience of others:

> I had no idea. You told us we were going to Gaza, to visit refugee camps and clinics, but I had no idea what that really meant. I have been to places of great poverty in Central America and Asia, but I have never experienced anything like this. I have always heard of Gaza, of course, but it is very different to walk in the refugee camps and to meet people who have virtually nothing, not even a reason to hope for a better economic or political future.

Gaza is one of the most densely populated areas on earth. This stretch of land, roughly 35 miles long and three to five miles across, is home for some 650,000 people, the vast majority of whom are Palestinian refugees displaced from their family homes in 1947–48. A small percentage of the population is from Gaza originally. Living conditions are awful. Economic opportunities are practically nonexistent. Massive assistance from outside — through United Nations agencies, church and other human service organizations, and other Palestinians in exile — is needed simply to keep the highly unpleasant status quo from worsening.

Such disparity in resources between the "haves" and the "have nots" breeds deep resentment. This is true both among and within the Middle Eastern states. The "have nots" hear a good deal of rhetoric concerning their economic and political plight. In most instances, however, those with the resources to help in tangible ways do very little.

Throughout the Middle East, as in most parts of the world, all-too-familiar patterns of opulent lifestyles and corruption at high levels in government further raise the level of anger and frustration among the populace. Nor should the power of this popular sentiment be underestimated. Anger at similar patterns of economic disparity and exploitation figured prominently in the downfall of the former Shah of Iran and of Ferdinand Marcos in the Philippines. Pictures of the shah's solid gold bathroom fixtures and Imelda Marcos's closets full of shoes became popular symbols of the excessive wealth of corrupt leaders. In the wake of the Gulf war, the ruling elites in Kuwait have seen clear signs of such popular discontent.

THE LESSONS OF WAR

Instability in the Middle East also fans outward from the unresolved regional conflicts. The multisided civil war in Lebanon, for example, has had a pervasive impact throughout the region. The changing alliances and interplay among recognized governments, nongovernmental groups and factions in Lebanon have been nothing short of bewildering over the past fifteen years. The short-hand term for these various interrelationships in the intricate web of regional politics is "linkage."

The interconnectedness of regional politics showed throughout the Gulf crisis. Immediately after his ill-conceived invasion of Kuwait, Saddam Hussein expressed willingness to withdraw if other occupying forces would do the same elsewhere in the Middle East. Specifically, he spoke of the quarter-century-long Israeli military occupation of the West Bank and Gaza and the fifteen-year-old Syrian military deployment in Lebanon. In other words, he challenged the international community with inconsistency in dealing with regional conflicts. His point struck a nerve.

While official U.S. policy rejected dealing with other regional conflicts to defuse the crisis, the political reality of "linkage" was unambiguous. When President Bush addressed the U.N. General Assembly in September 1990, he emphasized the centrality of regional conflicts as destabilizing factors. He also pledged to work vigorously for a settlement to the Israeli/Palestinian conflict once the Gulf crisis was resolved. The U.S.-led efforts to facilitate such a peace process in the immediate aftermath of the Gulf war added substance to these commitments.

Saddam Hussein understood and sought to exploit the political power of the Israeli/Palestinian conflict by joining it to his agenda. Within the first three days of the war, Iraq began firing SCUD missiles at Israeli cities in an effort to draw Israel into the conflict. Had he succeeded, Egypt, Saudi Arabia, Syria and other Middle Eastern nations aligned with the allied coalition opposing Iraq would have faced a major dilemma: alter their allegiance or be perceived as joining with Israel as well as the U.S. to fight another Arab state. Although Israel was not drawn in directly, the confrontation showed how interconnected regional conflicts help cause frustration and instability in the Middle East.

The Human Cost

The Gulf crisis highlighted the urgent need for tangible progress in the elusive search for peace. It also provided a window through which we could view other issues that pervade the region. The challenges facing people in the Middle East are substantial. So, too, are the challenges for others in the world community. Any hope for durable peace and stability requires action to address the root causes of unrest and fundamental injustices. In addition, the complex, interdependent nature of our world community means that systemic problems need multinational approaches. Some examples illustrate these points.

In the immediate aftermath of the war, the Kurds in northern Iraq (and the predominantly Shi'ite community in southern Iraq) revolted against Saddam Hussein. After initial success against the greatly weakened Iraqi army, the tables turned. Suddenly, the insurgents — who had been encouraged by President Bush to rise up and overthrow Iraq's leader — were being decimated by the Iraqi army. Much of the world looked on in horror as the Kurdish uprising was brutally put down and some two million Kurds fled through the mountains to seek safety in Turkey and Iran.

For two weeks the White House described the tragedy of the Kurdish people as "an internal Iraqi problem." Why? What made the ruthless slaughter of Kurds less horrific than the ruthless brutality visited on Kuwait? Borders. Iraq's takeover of another country provoked widespread international condemnation. The assault on Kurds inside Iraq produced only verbal condemnation since the Iraqi government forces had crossed no international border. Two weeks and many thousands of deaths later, the U.S. government, under enormous domestic pressure to stop Iraq's army and help the hapless refugees, mounted a major humanitarian response. At a certain point the technicalities of legal borders gave way to the moral necessity of responding to human beings in dire circumstances. The whole affair illustrated the dilemma of working within the constraints imposed by nation-state boundaries, even when the borders do not make sense.

The Gulf crisis also brought into the open the problem of systematic violation of basic human rights through oppressive political structures. Iraq received the most intense media scrutiny. News pages and the airwaves featured stories recounting Iraqi government atrocities, both in Kuwait and Iraq. The oppressive climate in which Iraqis have lived since Hussein seized power in 1979 was illuminated in

detail. The swift uprising among Kurds and southern Shi'ites immediately after the war showed what deep resentment and anger
such conditions have created. Although the descriptions were new
for most people in the West, those who follow events in the Middle
East closely were already well aware of the Iraqi leader's repressive
behavior. Why then did so many Middle Easterners support Iraq in
the war? Their support was based on his political positions and religious rhetoric. To deflect attention from his actions and rally outside
support, Hussein addressed deeply felt concerns of many people.
Most people who rallied behind him did so in spite of his abysmal
record of tyranny.

During the war Saddam Hussein's strategies included several
types of actions that horrified most people. Releasing several million gallons of crude oil into the sea and setting ablaze some five
hundred oil wells in Kuwait deliberately wreaked havoc on the environment. Firing SCUD missiles at Israel and Saudi Arabia amounted
to indiscriminate attacks on civilians. Civilians almost always suffer directly from war. But the attacks are not usually so blatantly
directed at noncombatants.

The revulsion evoked by Saddam Hussein's military tactics and
human rights abuses was both understandable and appropriate. Such
behavior is, to put it mildly, intolerable. Will government leaders and
a concerned public collectively express outrage over other unspeakable abuses in the world? Will the resolve to halt tyranny, oppression
and human rights abuses motivate constructive multinational policy
decisions in the future?

The Gulf war has taught us that the world community can and
must find collective political and economic ways to stop aggression,
exploitation and brutality. War is not the answer, nor was it in the
eyes of many the "only" option in the Gulf crisis. While human
casualties on the allied side were remarkably few, we must not be
naive about the terrible costs of war. The numbers of dead and injured in Iraq may never be known with accuracy. Within the first
six months after the war, however, estimates in the *New York Times*
placed the figure at 150,000. And health officials visiting postwar
Iraq reported on the continuing loss of life from disease, malnutri-
tion and lack of medical care — all direct results of the devastation
of Iraq's infrastructure. Many other costs of war, even a "successful"
one, may not be visible or known for years. The economic impact
is far-reaching. No one can measure the influence of this catastro-
phe on the next generation of Arabs and their neighbors; the seeds

for extremism have been sown. How much the extremism grows depends, in large part, on what happens next in the region. No one yet knows if or how much this war will serve, in the end, to destabilize further an already unstable region.

Oil Resources and Global Economics

The Gulf crisis further showed the urgency of dealing cooperatively with the global need for oil and the reality of economic interdependence. A closer look at these issues will help us understand what people and nations in the Middle East — and the rest of the world — are facing.

Without question, oil was a central factor in the Gulf crisis. With the capture of Kuwait, Saddam Hussein suddenly controlled massive oil production facilities and 25 percent of the world's known oil reserves. Soon many leaders were expressing fears that the Iraqi leader also had designs on the oil fields of Saudi Arabia. Two weeks into the crisis, President Bush identified the dangers posed by Saddam Hussein's potential control of such oil reserves: "Our jobs, our way of life, our freedom and the freedom of friendly countries around the world would all suffer" (*New York Times*, Aug. 16, 1990).

Within hours of the Iraqi invasion of Kuwait, stock markets plummeted worldwide in anticipation of lower supply and higher oil prices. For weeks thereafter, the markets in Bonn, London, Tokyo and New York gyrated unpredictably. By November, oil prices had stabilized, although at levels significantly higher than before Iraq's invasion, and stock markets began to regroup.

In North America, sobering realities set in. Canada and the U.S. have extraordinarily high rates of per capita consumption of oil. Both countries are deeply dependent on imported oil. The necessity to reduce consumption and vigorously explore alternative and renewable sources of energy was affirmed, as it had been in 1973 and 1978 when oil embargos and major price increases created long lines at gas stations and, more significantly, triggered cycles of inflation and unemployment throughout the economies. Complacency returned during the 1980s. Between 1985 and 1990, oil consumption rose rapidly. In early 1990, import levels reached their highest mark since 1979. The unlearned lessons of the 1970s were back before us in 1990–91.

Throughout this century oil and political power have been intimately linked. Daniel Yergin's 1991 book, *The Prize: The Epic Quest*

for Oil, Money and Power, convincingly documents this link. Poised
on the brink of a new century, we now need more urgently than ever
to face reality squarely. Global dependence on oil is a fact of life —
at least for the foreseeable future. The Gulf crisis has reminded us
all — especially the major consumers of fossil fuels — that we must
be far more diligent in our efforts to conserve energy, reduce consumption and explore alternative sources of energy that are reliable,
safe and renewable.

The fact that oil is currently so closely tied to economic structures
presents real challenges and real dangers. The entire world has a
vested interest in a stable, predictable and affordable supply of oil.
Thus the whole world has a vital interest in the Gulf region where
a large portion of the known oil reserves is located. Vigorous efforts
in the community of nations are needed to understand better the
nature of our economic interdependence and to explore cooperatively
ways to defuse this ticking bomb. Complacency and miscalculations
about stability can have far-reaching consequences, particularly in an
interdependent world that is heavily armed.

The Middle East Arms Race

Perhaps the most sobering lessons from the Gulf war have to do
with sales and transfers of weapons systems. The burgeoning international arms industry thrives in the Middle East. Per capita, the
nations in this strategically important region are the most heavily
armed in the world. The Gulf crisis provided a crash course on these
unsettling realities.

The scale of arms sales and the proliferation of weapons systems
during the past thirty years has been staggering. The percentage of
national budgets devoted to military expenditures in many Middle
Eastern nations increases every year. The American Friends Service
Committee's Peace Education Division has monitored arms sales and
transfers for years. The Quaker-based organization characterized the
situation in the Middle East in a bulletin issued in the summer of
1991:

> From 1979 to 1988 alone, Middle Eastern nations imported
> more than $150 billion worth of arms, approximately half the
> arms exported to the Third World. Israel, Egypt and Turkey
> also produce much of their own weapons. Iraq, Egypt, Syria
> and Israel each have more than half a million troops.... Several
> Middle Eastern nations spend 20 percent or more of the GNP

on military forces; the world average is approximately 5.5 percent.*

Military sales is a very lucrative business, one in which annual expenditures are measured in billions of dollars. From 1982 to 1989 Saudi Arabia and Iraq spent $44 and $43 billion on weapons, respectively. The 1990 report to the U.S. Congress indicated that U.S. arms sales to the Middle East that year ($33 billion) represented two-thirds of its total foreign sales of arms.

During the Gulf crisis, we learned that Iraq was a prime customer in the Middle East arms bazaar. The dangers posed by a well-armed despot with visions of empire suddenly came sharply into focus. Iraq, a nation of 18 million people, boasted of an army numbering one million. How did Iraq get to this point? Are there any safeguards to prevent Saddam Hussein or some other leader from obtaining whatever weapons are desired?

Arms for the Buying   The global arms market has had far too little scrutiny. In fact, all the major arms-producing nations — the U.S., the U.S.S.R., France, Great Britain and the People's Republic of China head the list — had been selling billions of dollars in weapons to Iraq throughout the 1980s. In short, "we" are very much part of the problem. Supplying the region with expensive, sophisticated weapons may yield short-term fiscal benefits. In the medium and long run, however, such virtually unregulated behavior is foolish. It puts much of the world, including ourselves, at risk. The populace within these highly militarized societies is also bound to be affected. And in a region where alliances change with great frequency, who can presume to control the movement or use of these deadly weapons?

The fluid way arms move around in the region was made real to me during a 1984 visit in Lebanon. Three of us were invited to Lebanon for meetings with religious and political leaders. As we traveled through various sections of Beirut, the Bekaa Valley and portions of southern Lebanon, we were stopped at numerous militia checkpoints. The wide array of American, Soviet and French-made weaponry we could see astonished us. No particular pattern seemed to prevail; every militia had weapons from every major supplier.

One afternoon in downtown West Beirut, I passed a thirteen- or

---

*For information on the AFSC's publications, write AFSC, Peace Education Division, 1501 Cherry Street, Philadelphia, PA 19102.

Arms and the Middle East

Where Arms Come From:

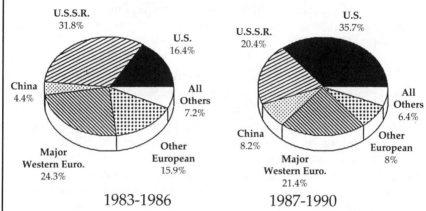

1983-1986   1987-1990

Percentage of Arms Transfers to the Middle East

Where U.S. Arms Transfers Go:

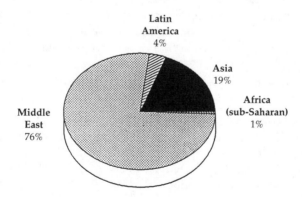

New Transfer Agreements, 1987-90

Source: Congressional Research Service
Charts courtesy of Council for a Livable World

fourteen-year-old boy as he swaggered down the sidewalk with a brand new American-made automatic rifle. Stunned and angered, I asked my Lebanese colleague, "How can a young Shi'ite boy get hold of such sophisticated U.S.-made weapons? Isn't he in a militia group hostile to the stated U.S. government positions in Lebanon?" With a shrug and a somewhat patronizing smile, my companion reminded me that "the U.S. government is not too discriminating when it comes to selling weapons." He paused, then added, "Anyone can get practically any weapon in this region. So long as you have the money to pay for it, your political positions are of little consequence."

Many concerned citizens in the U.S. and Canada have argued for years that the profit-driven pattern of global arms sales was both immoral and exceedingly dangerous. Flooding the Middle East with weapons and then proclaiming surprise or anger when despotic leaders use the weapons in ways "we" don't like falls somewhere between hypocrisy and naiveté. When pressed on these points, many legislators and government officials in the U.S., France, Great Britain and other arms-producing countries have denied being hypocritical or naive. Instead, they have insisted that the arms sales practices were "realistic:" "If we don't sell arms, someone else will!"

Postwar Initiatives   This overused, self-serving excuse may yet give way to concerted, multilateral approaches to curb the flow of arms to the Middle East. President Bush included arms control on the postwar agenda during his speech to a joint session of the U.S. Congress one week after the formal cessation of the Gulf war. "It would be tragic," Bush said, "if a new arms race were to begin in the Middle East." In May 1991, at the Air Force Academy commencement, Bush outlined parts of his plan to halt the spread of weapons of mass destruction:

> We are committed to stopping the proliferation of weapons of mass destruction. . . . Halting the proliferation of conventional and unconventional weapons in the Middle East — while supporting the legitimate need of every state to defend itself — will require the cooperation of many states, in the region and around the world. It won't be easy — but the path to peace never is. . . . I am today proposing a Middle East arms control initiative. It features supplier guidelines on conventional arms exports, barriers to exports that contribute to weapons of mass

destruction, a freeze now and later a ban on surface-to-surface missiles in the region and a ban on nuclear weapons material.*

President Bush also called for a conference of the five leading supplier states — the U.S., U.S.S.R., France, Great Britain and China — to set guidelines curbing arms sales. The first round of discussions was held in London during August 1991. In addition to the top five arms suppliers, representatives from several other Western powers were present. While these preliminary conversations produced little tangible progress, there were encouraging signs. The Canadian government, for instance, argued strongly against the arms bazaar. It will surely take the concerted effort of many countries to push for meaningful changes in this destructive pattern of behavior.

Whatever comes of President Bush's postwar initiative, it has served to put critical issues on the table. The old ways of "doing business" are unacceptable for a host of reasons. Concerned people of faith, particularly those living in countries that produce and peddle the armaments, must monitor what is happening in their lands as well as what is being said and done by government officials. We are all part of the problem. And if the headlong rush toward new wars is left unchecked, we will all be victims of the conflagrations.

Another major item, perhaps the major item, on the postwar agenda is the Israeli/Palestinian conflict. Most major leaders — President Bush, Canada's Prime Minister Mulrooney, Britain's Prime Minister John Major, France's President Mitterand, Soviet President Gorbachev and others — have affirmed that any hope for lasting peace and stability in the region requires meaningful progress toward resolving this longstanding conflict. Accordingly, U.S. Secretary of State James Baker devoted considerable energy to this problem for many months after the Gulf war. We turn now to a closer look at this pivotal and tragic conflict.

---

*"Bush Unveils Plan for Arms Control in the Middle East," *New York Times*, May 30, 1991.

THE ISRAELI/PALESTINIAN CONFLICT

The Israeli/Palestinian conflict remains the most pervasive and destabilizing element in the Middle East. Resolving this conflict would not bring peace to the region since, as we have noted earlier, there are many sources of unrest and instability. But it would accomplish several critical goals. It would end the tragic suffering experienced by both Israelis and Palestinians for over half a century. It would remove a major factor complicating other issues in the region. It would also provide hope for positive movement on other seemingly intractable problems. And it would ease the world community back from the brink of a wider confrontation.

The contemporary conflict, while rooted in history, is largely a twentieth-century phenomenon. We have already seen how Western powers played a pivotal and confusing role while the conflict developed. It comes as no surprise to discover that Jews and Arabs often have different perceptions of the history that brings them to this juncture. Both communities have suffered and both have viable claims to their place in this sacred land. Many Palestinians have viewed Jewish settlement and the creation of Israel as an intrusion into the area. Many Israeli Jews, on the other hand, have refused to recognize the rights of the indigenous Palestinians as a people with a distinct identity and legitimate claims to their homeland. A superb study, *A Compassionate Peace: A Future for Israel, Palestine, and the Middle East,* makes clear, more than one truth is operative this unique land:

> While a remnant of the ancient Jewish community remained in the Holy Land through the centuries, active Jewish settlement began in the late nineteenth century, guided by a new social movement. This movement, Zionism, was in part a response to the pogroms carried out against the Jews of Europe. The attempt to bring Jews to the Holy Land after centuries of living in the diaspora was very much a political event, reaffirming the land of Palestine as the Jewish homeland. Migration, increasing into the 1930s, exploded when World War II and the Holocaust made the homeland a haven vital for Jewish survival. What did not enter deeply enough into the consciousness of the early twentieth-century settlers was the extent to which their national aspirations conflicted with legitimate Arab claims to the same land. The need to resettle the hundreds of thousands of Jew-

ish refugees from Europe pushed such awareness even further into the background. Few thought to ask the other residents in the land, the Arabs, how to resolve the desperate need of the refugees. To ask today whether the Jewish refugees could have been settled differently is to engage in nonproductive discussion. To ask now how to reconcile the needs of two peoples within the same area can lead to innovative solutions.*

The Israelis and Palestinians, the protagonists, must play the major roles in the effort to achieve peace. The particular history of this conflict also means that others have parts to play as well. A durable peace requires reconciliation between Israel and the neighboring Arab states. Most analysts agree that this delicate "peace process" will need the strong support of the international community. The U.S. and U.S.S.R., the Europeans and/or the member states of the U.N. Security Council will be needed to provide a structure, help build trust and guarantee security for the wary participants in the "peace process." Meeting the challenge will demand multinational cooperation and a level of patience, resolve, courage, creativity and perseverance rarely displayed in the political arena.

When the political will exists, negotiated settlements can be found. In broad terms, a workable peace will require accommodation on land or territorial compromise, mutual recognition, affirmations of self-determination and provisions for perceived security needs. A closer look at these elements points to obstacles and opportunities that lie ahead.

Land

Land is at the center of the dispute. Both Israelis and Palestinians present credible and compelling claims for a homeland in Israel/Palestine. Recognizing the needs and rights of both communities, the U.N. General Assembly adopted Resolution 181 in 1947, setting forth a plan for partitioning the area under British mandate into two independent states. Resolution 181 specified plans for the transition, new governance and economic cooperation. The months leading to the full implementation of the plan were tumultuous. The majority of Israeli Jews accepted the plan; the Arab majority did not. Rather than two states being born in 1948, war erupted. Tens of thousands of Palestinian refugees fled north into Lebanon and Syria, east into

---

*Everett Mendelsohn, *A Compassionate Peace: A Future for Israel, Palestine, and the Middle East*, rev. ed. (New York: Hill and Wang, 1989), p. 23.

Jordan and south into the Gaza district. Israel's victory expanded into the lands set apart for the new Arab state in Palestine.

In the wake of the 1948 war, Arab territory in Palestine was placed under the control of Jordan (the West Bank of the Jordan River, including East Jerusalem) and Egypt (Gaza). This division of territory and control continued for twenty years, interrupted by several major and numerous local clashes. The status changed dramatically, however, after the June 1967 Arab-Israeli war. Israel's swift, decisive victory brought the West Bank, Gaza and the Golan Heights (Syrian territory) under Israeli control. Five months after the 1967 war, the U.N. Security Council unanimously adopted the now famous Resolution 242. The first article in this resolution sets forth key principles required for the establishment of a just and lasting peace:

> (i) Withdrawal of Israeli armed forces from territories occupied in the recent conflict; (ii) Termination of all claims or states of belligerency and respect for and acknowledgement of the sovereignty, territorial integrity and political independence of every state in the area and their right to live in peace within secure and recognized boundaries free from threats or acts of force.

Resolution 242 presents a "land for peace" formula, a principle that has been available now for twenty-five years. Unfortunately, the degree to which the Israelis, Palestinians and Arab states have been willing to embrace this formula has fluctuated. When the Israelis were more predisposed to accept the compromise, the Palestinians and other Arabs were not. In the 1980s, when the Palestinian position evolved toward a "land for peace" settlement, Israel's Likud or Likud-Labor coalition governments became more set against giving up any of the territories they have occupied since the 1967 war.

In fact, Israeli leaders, beginning with the first term of Prime Minister Menachem Begin in 1977, have stopped referring to the "Occupied Territories" and speak instead of "Judea and Samaria." Further, they have actively promoted the establishment of Jewish settlements in the Occupied Territories. Yitzhak Shamir, the Israeli Prime Minister for much of the 1980s, has remained steadfast in his belief that Israel has a right to settle in and permanently control Judea and Samaria. He, and others, have declared repeatedly that they would never give up "one inch of Eretz Israel" (the land of Israel).

The policy of building settlements has complicated further an already complex situation. At the beginning of 1992, the number of settlers in the West Bank, Gaza and Golan Heights has surpassed 100,000 (another 120,000 Israeli Jews live in settlements in and around East Jerusalem); they live in approximately 200 settlements; they control more than 50 percent of the land as well as the large majority of water resources. The settlements have "created new facts" on the ground, thus making a negotiated "land for peace" agreement much more difficult.

Barriers to Peace

Political dynamics are another complicating factor. Among those who settled the West Bank and Gaza in the past quarter-century, the large majority belong to the Gush Emunim (Block of the Faithful). The members of this group are ideologically and theologically committed to a vision of Israel that precludes any type of land compromise in a negotiated settlement. Substantial numbers of settlers have been involved in violent actions directed against the local Arabs. While the actual number of settlers remains small — only 5–7 percent of the Israeli electorate — the political power and influence of the extremists has grown dramatically in Israel in the past two decades. In a fascinating study of Jewish fundamentalism in Israel, *For the Land and the Lord*, Ian Lustick summarizes the growth of Gush Emunim as of 1988:

> Fairly radical fundamentalist beliefs, attitudes, and political programs that were regarded as crackpot extremism by the vast majority of Israelis in the late 1960s (for example, destroying Muslim shrines in Jerusalem, rebuilding the Temple before the Messiah comes, or forming Jewish terrorist groups to strike at local Arabs) appear to be embraced by approximately 20 percent of the Israeli Jewish population. About 30–35 percent of Israeli Jews are now willing to associate themselves with related policies and beliefs (such as agreement with policies of subjugation and expulsion for Arabs and opposition to any freeze on the establishment of new settlements).*

In May 1991 U.S. Secretary of State James Baker unambiguously described the barriers to peace raised by the ongoing Israeli settlement process and the accompanying political positions. After five

---

*Ian Lustick, *For the Land and the Lord: Jewish Fundamentalism in Israel* (Washington, D.C.: Council on Foreign Relations, 1988), p. 15.

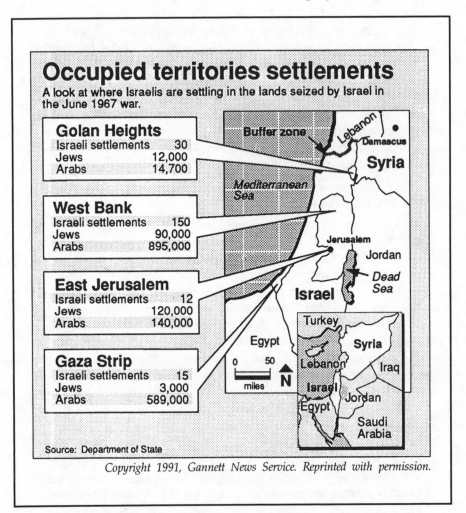

Occupied territories settlements

A look at where Israelis are settling in the lands seized by Israel in the June 1967 war.

Golan Heights
Israeli settlements	30
Jews	12,000
Arabs	14,700

West Bank
Israeli settlements	150
Jews	90,000
Arabs	895,000

East Jerusalem
Israeli settlements	12
Jews	120,000
Arabs	140,000

Gaza Strip
Israeli settlements	15
Jews	3,000
Arabs	589,000

Buffer zone · Lebanon · Damascus · Syria

Mediterranean Sea

Jerusalem · Jordan · Dead Sea · Israel

Egypt

0   50
miles   N

Turkey · Syria · Lebanon · Iraq · Israel · Jordan · Egypt · Saudi Arabia

Source: Department of State

Copyright 1991, Gannett News Service. Reprinted with permission.

trips through the Middle East following the Gulf war, Baker reported to the Congress concerning progress on an Israeli/Palestinian peace process. Expressing his frustration, Baker lamented, "I don't think there is any bigger obstacle to peace than the settlement activity." When Baker and President Bush were pressed on this point, both strongly reaffirmed longstanding U.S. policy against settlement in occupied lands.

Approaches to peace and the obstacles blocking progress depend, in part, on what kind of solution is envisioned. Continuing settlements appear to preclude the most promising solutions, such as an independent Palestinian state (in the West Bank and Gaza) or a Palestinian entity in confederation with Jordan and/or Israel. The extremist policies of settlers envision another kind of "solution," namely: formal Israeli annexation of occupied lands or the so-called Jordanian option (expulsion of most Palestinians into Jordan where, according to this "option," they could establish their state).

On the surface, the prospects for compromise appear slim. Yet we must remember that the majority of Israelis deeply desire peace and have expressed repeatedly in polls their willingness to trade land for peace if (and it is a big "if") they were sure a genuine peace was achievable. Many still point to the dramatic developments of 1977 and 1978 — Egyptian President Anwar Sadat's surprise trip to Jerusalem and the subsequent Camp David peace accords — as a reminder that positions deemed impossible quickly became possible when political circumstances changed and a new level of trust was established.

The lack of trust on all sides is understandable; it is also a major barrier to meaningful progress. Both sides must find ways to build trust with their adversaries. Clear positions that recognize and affirm the de facto existence and rights of both communities are needed. "Mutual recognition" and the right of "self-determination" are the terms most often used to express these requirements.

Mutual Recognition

For decades, most Palestinians and most Arab states refused to recognize Israel's very existence, viewing it as a kind of colonial settler state foisted upon the Arabs by Westerners in the wake of the Holocaust. This attitude, combined with violent confrontation, obviously has deepened Israeli suspicion about Arab sincerity in any peace process. Conversely, a substantial portion of Israelis have rejected the very idea of a Palestinian national identity with political rights in a Palestinian state. This view, combined with well-documented repressive policies toward Palestinians during 25 years of military occupation, has similarly undercut the effort to build and nurture trust.

The difficulty of achieving mutual recognition was illustrated in the 1991 shuttle diplomacy of James Baker. Israeli leaders refused to accept, even in principle, that the Palestinians had the right to identify their own representatives in a negotiation process. Israel pressed for direct talks with individual Arab states, but remained adamantly opposed to dealing even indirectly with the Palestine Liberation Organization (PLO). Arab states and the Palestinians, on the other hand, wanted a broader peace process under U.N. or joint U.S.-U.S.S.R. auspices. They pushed for a structure that recognized Palestinian rights from the outset. What appeared in the media to be a kind of procedural hang-up, was a reflection of the deeper problems: lack of trust, the need for mutual recognition and affirmation of rights of self-determination.

A broad consensus in the international community favors a settlement based on the "land for peace" formula in U.N. Resolution 242. For this to succeed, all parties will need strong guarantees on the second principle of that resolution: "...their right to live in peace within secure and recognized boundaries free from the threats or acts of force."

Security

In essence, for trust to begin, hostilities must cease and security guarantees for all peoples must be put in place. Israelis readily identify the security issue as a top priority. Although Israel has by far the most sophisticated military capability in the region, the people still feel insecure. Many point to the map, note Israel's precarious position and remind others that "Israel cannot afford to lose one war." In view of their turbulent history this century and the longer history of persecution endured by the Jews, the desire for iron-clad guarantees of security is surely understandable.

Palestinians also need clearly defined security guarantees. They, too, have suffered as refugees — in their homeland and abroad — and as people living under military occupation. The Palestinians rightly point out that they have lived as insecure and vulnerable people for decades. In view of their history, they also need more than verbal assurances that their basic rights will be protected in whatever political entity comes into being. Specific measures, such as buffer zones or U.N. peacekeeping forces, will need to be worked out in the "peace process."

Security concerns moved to a new level during the Gulf war. Both the Israeli Jews and the Palestinian Arabs are less secure because of the expanding and increasingly sophisticated military technology present in the region. Strategically placed conventional troops can no longer provide security against weapons of mass destruction such as missiles and chemical, biological and possibly nuclear weaponry. Indeed, powerful weapons that threaten others cannot produce genuine security. The best way to enhance security is not with larger expenditures on weapons. Security, in the end, must rest on a recognition of the mutuality of interests.

Any comprehensive settlement will also have to deal with other unresolved issues. Wide disagreements exist, for example, on the rights of and reparations due refugees and displaced persons. The status of Jerusalem is also a major obstacle blocking the way toward peace. Should the city be divided? Can it be the capital for two states? Could Jerusalem be a special kind of "international" city? The deep attachments to this unique city raise everyone's emotional stakes. Most analysts agree that the status of Jerusalem should be addressed as one of the final agenda items in a comprehensive negotiation process. Otherwise, emotions may well short-circuit the entire peace process.

The nature and history of the conflict suggest that the road ahead will not be easy. No party will get everything it wants or feels entitled to receive. Major compromises will be required if the parties to the conflict hope to achieve even a proximate measure of justice. Yet good reasons for hope exist.

REASONS FOR HOPE

During the Gulf crisis and immediately after the Gulf war, the community of nations agreed that a peaceful settlement of the Israeli/Palestinian conflict is necessary. This conviction was visible even in the politically divided Middle East. Alliances formed during the Gulf crisis produced a broader consensus among many Arab states and the U.S.-led coalition. Renewed efforts to resolve this ongoing conflict were called for and undertaken, most notably in the shuttle diplomacy pursued by James Baker. Whatever interruptions characterize peace efforts in the months after the Gulf war, a consensus has developed: an Israeli/Palestinian peace settlement is the priority in the Middle East.

A second and all-important reason for hope is that the large majority of Israelis and Palestinians deeply desire peace. Although groups differ widely on what would constitute a genuine peace and how best to achieve it, most people recognize that the situation cannot remain as it is. As we all witnessed in the 1977–78 Israeli-Egyptian peace process, hardline positions can soften and adversaries may be willing to take limited risks for peace when the circumstances change. The voices of those who have long advocated accommodation through a negotiated settlement have become more audible in the wake of the Gulf war.*

There are many signs of hope within Israel. During the war triggered by the 1982 Israeli invasion of Lebanon, for example, 500,000 Israelis poured into the streets to protest aspects of their government's military policies, including efforts to conceal complicity in the massacre of over 1,000 Palestinians in the Sabra and Shatila refugee camps near Beirut. Throughout the 1980s, a variety of groups — from the broad-based Peace Now to more narrowly focused civil and human rights organizations — have pressed for negotiations to resolve the entrenched problems.

National elections in Israel during the 1980s revealed a society deeply divided. Twice the two major parties, Labor and Likud, had to resort to awkward coalition government arrangements because neither could form the majority necessary to run the government.

---

*Two collections of interviews, published by Friendship Press in 1987 and 1991, convey the range of views and the depth of concern for peace on both sides: *Unified in Hope: Arabs and Jews Talk About Peace*, and *Justice and the Intifada: Palestinians and Israelis Speak Out*.

While it seems that the more conservative forces, led by Yitzhak Shamir and the Likud Block, have the numerical advantage, the opinion polls in Israel have continued to show that the majority of Israelis would support some type of "land for peace" negotiated settlement. A considerable gap exists, however, between this approach and any agreement on the details.

In the midst of the Gulf war, when SCUD missiles were falling on Israel in late January 1991, the Israeli peace movement was in disarray. Many peace activists were discouraged and angry at the widely perceived Palestinian support for Iraq. Even during this low-point, however, *The Nation* magazine reported a poll indicating that 44.7 percent of the Israeli public explicitly favored negotiations with the PLO.

Political Initiatives

On the Palestinian side, significant changes during the past five years have created hope for the eventual resolution of the conflict. Without question, the Palestinian *intifadah* ("uprising") has been the catalyst for these changes. Recognizing that no outside power was going to resolve the conflict, Palestinians in Gaza and the West Bank joined in a spontaneous and remarkably unified protest against Israeli occupation beginning in early December 1987. Stepping up various protest actions that they had used sporadically for years — commercial strikes, boycotts, public demonstrations, confronting Israeli soldiers — Palestinians discovered a new strength in their unity. And, for the first time, the world media focused on their sustained protests in daily coverage. Palestinian resolve strengthened as they discovered growing support around the world.

A striking feature of the intifadah has been the democratic dialogue among Palestinians. The overwhelming majority have always supported the PLO (through its various factions). But prior to the intifadah, West Bank and Gaza Palestinians largely followed the guidance of Palestinian leaders in exile. Since 1987, however, strategy and policy debates go back and forth. Perhaps the most telling indication of the change came at the 1988 Palestine National Council (PNC) meeting in Algiers.

The PNC decision to declare an independent Palestinian state alongside Israel represented a major shift of the PLO toward accommodation and moderation. For years many within the PLO had been moving toward a two-state solution. But many Palestinians who

THE PALESTINIAN LIBERATION ORGANIZATION

The Palestinian Liberation Organization (PLO) was founded at a meeting of Arab heads of state in January, 1964.... The PLO's basic constitution vests supreme power in determining PLO policy in a body called the Palestinian National Council (PNC), which has acted with increasing effectiveness since 1964 as a kind of Palestinian parliament-in-exile. The PNC representatives come from various militia groups, Palestinian "mass organisations" for students, workers, women... representatives from various refugee communities and geographical areas....

One of the PNC's main tasks, in addition to laying down the broad lines of PLO policy, has been to elect the PLO's ruling Executive Committee. In practice this has always been accomplished through protracted negotiations among the different PLO groupings, before and during each PNC session.... Since 1969, Yasser Arafat, the head of Fateh (the largest Palestinian group within the PLO), has served as the Chairman of the PLO's ruling Executive Committee....

In addition to its political organs, the PLO has been able to develop various other aspects of a quasi-state form of organisation. It commands its own regular army (as distinct from the individual forces established by the various guerrilla groups).... On the purely civilian side, the PLO created a whole series of institutions which sought to tie the Organisation directly into many aspects of Palestinian life. The Palestinian Red Crescent Society built and operates a whole network of modern hospitals... as well as running clinics in many refugee camps.

The Sons of Martyrs Society, Samed, started off as an orphan-aid project, but rapidly grew to comprise large and modern factories in many manufacturing fields including textiles, carpentry, metalwork and film processing.... Funding for the activities above has come from the Palestinian National Fund, set up alongside the PLO in 1964 for this purpose. While the PNF continues to collect the income tax from Palestinians living in Arab countries... its major source of funding from the mid-60s on was the direct subventions from the Arab governments paid directly to the PLO under the provisions of successive Arab summit meetings.

From Helena Cobban, The Palestinian Liberation Organisation: People, Power and Politics *(Cambridge: Cambridge University Press, 1984), pp. 10–14.*

originally lived in Jaffa, Haifa or other places within the 1948–1967 boundaries of Israel did not agree. And some among the Palestinians have always resisted any accommodation with Israel. The strong message of the intifadah moved the process forward. Palestinians living alongside Israelis had come to terms with coexistence. These Palestinians stressed that the time had now come to accept what they viewed as partial justice as the only realistic way to achieve self-determination and fulfill the desires for a nation of their own.

Specifically, the PNC declared the existence of a Palestinian state, citing U.N. Resolution 181 as the legitimate birth certificate. This resolution, as we noted earlier, included the original partition plan for two states. Four decades later, the Palestinians declared that the legitimacy of their state rests on the same international basis as does that of Israel. Next, the PNC looked to 1967 and U.N. Resolution 242 to define the boundaries for the two states. Finally, the PNC called for an international conference under U.N. auspices to provide the framework within which to work out the many difficult issues.

These actions, together with PLO leader Yassir Arafat's November 1988 speech to the United Nations in Geneva, clarified the PNC's positions. These developments and Arafat's statement renouncing the use of terrorism provided the U.S. government with a rationale to shift the policy it has followed since 1975 when then Secretary of State Henry Kissinger set conditions for meeting with the PLO. In December 1988, U.S. officials met openly with PLO officials in Tunisia to begin a substantive dialogue.

The Challenge of Peace

This new momentum for peace through a negotiated settlement subsequently ebbed for several reasons. Lack of substantial progress produced growing frustration among Palestinians. New incidents of violence inside and outside Israel renewed distrust and deepened the ambivalence already present. Then, when the international community was most needed to nurture the process, other events took over the world stage. In 1989, global attention understandably shifted toward the dramatic developments in Eastern Europe and the Soviet Union. As previously unthinkable political changes in socialist countries were happening daily, the Israelis and Palestinians settled back into an all too familiar pattern. The U.S. government, citing PLO complicity in acts of violence, suspended the dialogue with the PLO.

Internal problems grew among Palestinians. Moderate voices were challenged by more extremist ones on the grounds that efforts at compromise and negotiation had produced little. An extremist Islamic group, Hamas, built its influence, particularly in Gaza. In addition, violence by Palestinians against other Palestinians perceived as collaborating with Israel began to rise sharply. The Gulf crisis and war made the deteriorating situation worsen. Responding to Saddam Hussein's rhetoric concerning their cause, many Palestinians openly supported the Iraqi leader. The deep frustration of people living for decades under oppressive conditions was manifest in highly unproductive ways. Media attention on those Palestinians who cheered the SCUD missile attacks on Israel, for instance, served primarily to harden positions and deepen fears among Israelis.

In 1992, the dynamics are different from those of early 1989. The Gulf war has both deepened the animosity between Arabs and Israelis and provided an impetus for pursuing a durable peace process. Nevertheless, it is important to remember the shifts in position that have occurred. The essential ingredients are present: the desire for peace remains strong; the international community appears committed to a peace process; the need for security and self-determination for both parties is widely affirmed. The challenge involves finding ways to develop trust and providing an environment in which all parties are able to take limited risks for peace.

The Need for Visible Progress

The 1990s will be crucial in the history of this tragic conflict. Substantial, constructive progress toward a peace settlement is possible; a relapse into an ever deeper and more bitter division looms as well. Unless the political processes produce some visible signs of hope, the frustration level among individuals and groups will grow and again erupt into more destabilizing, violent episodes.

In July 1989, for instance, a young man from Gaza jumped from his seat on an Israeli bus traveling from Tel Aviv to Jerusalem, grabbed the steering wheel and deliberately plunged the bus off the road into a deep ravine. Fifteen people died in the crash; many others were seriously injured. Both Israelis and Palestinians condemned this horrific act of violence, though the two communities interpreted it differently. The lead editorial in the *Jerusalem Post* of July 12, 1989, proclaimed, "Israel Aboard Bus 405," and depicted the episode as a concrete symbol of what Israelis fear daily. How, many

Israelis asked, can Israel be expected to make peace with people who want to destroy them?

Many Palestinians, however, saw the event as understandable in context. Some suggested it was even a "predictable" response by an individual who could no longer endure seeing friends and loved ones humiliated, beaten, shot or imprisoned on a daily basis in Gaza. Many Palestinians wondered aloud why more individuals had not "snapped" under the severe pressures created by decades of military occupation.

Israelis and Palestinians agreed that the traumatic event foreshadowed a future that nobody wants. At the same time, most recognize that the status quo is leading to that future. If there is no substantial progress toward peace, then more cycles of violence are likely — whether they center on an individual lashing out in some wanton act or an external group organizing a military strike or a band of vigilante settlers assaulting unarmed Palestinians on the very lands their families have inhabited for centuries.

Palestinians have watched the dramatic political changes in Eastern Europe. They also have watched as Nelson Mandela was released from prison in South Africa and the difficult political dialogue began in earnest. Palestinians recognize that political changes in the Middle East also will be difficult and require major concessions. But the fragile peace process must show visible signs that diplomacy and negotiation can work. Otherwise, extremist elements will find more and more people receptive to their appeals for violence.

New and unpredictable developments increase the need for tangible political progress. First, large numbers of Soviet and Ethiopian Jews are immigrating annually to Israel. Over 300,000 Soviet Jews arrived in Israel from 1989 through 1991. Freedom for these Jews is welcome news for all people of goodwill. But their arrival in Israel in such large numbers could create major problems. Israeli officials estimate that one million more Soviet Jews will arrive in Israel between 1992 and 1995. This large influx prompted the Israeli government to request $10 billion in loan guarantees from the U.S. government in September 1991. The U.S. decided to delay consideration until January 1992, in order to focus on the peace process and seek to resolve differences over Israeli settlement policies in the Occupied Territories.

Within the pre-1967 Israeli borders, the burgeoning numbers of Jewish emigrés will change the demographic picture markedly. Israeli Arabs — both Christians and Muslims — currently number about 700,000, or roughly 20 percent of the Israeli population. Their access to the Israeli political processes, already limited, will continue to diminish as their percentage in relation to the Jewish majority shrinks. Further, scarce resources, especially land and water, will be strained even more. Many of the 1.7 million West Bank and Gaza Palestinians fear that efforts to incorporate Soviet Jews will lead to increased settlement activity in the territories under military occupation, or, at the very least, to further confiscation of scarce resources.

The Gulf war added its own complications. It is too soon to say how deep are the wounds created from the harsh rhetoric and the missile attacks. This much is clear: the breach between those who were most willing to talk to their perceived adversaries — the moderates and peace activists on both sides — may widen further unless focused, short-term efforts to restore some measure of trust are successful.

The international community must move forthrightly into this delicate situation. The Israelis, Palestinians and other Arabs need the concerted best efforts of the community of nations. Painstaking work is required to build trust, provide security guarantees and construct a viable framework for pursuing a nonviolent settlement. The formal opening of a Middle East peace process in Madrid on October 30, 1991, has provided a much-needed sign of hope. The early phases of this initiative, sponsored jointly by the U.S. and the U.S.S.R., also have made clear that Middle East peacemaking will likely take several years to achieve.

Citizens in North America can play a substantial role in the process of peacemaking. We turn, finally, to an exploration of specific ways people of faith and goodwill can become part of the solution to this and other conflicts in the Middle East. There are no quick fixes. But there are many ways concerned North American Christians can become involved in productive and responsible efforts.

4

Responsible Ministry and Citizenship

MUTUAL MINISTRY

The call to responsible ministry in relation to the Middle East moves at several levels. Christians are linked with the people, places and events in these historic lands through the biblical tradition, the history of the church and, most recently, through developments in contemporary ecumenical relations. These strong ties impose a responsibility for prudent and persevering action together with the Christians in the Middle East.

At the same time, North American Christians are citizens in democratic societies whose policies shape world events. This, too, creates opportunities and imposes responsibilities. Silent acquiescence in the face of whatever government officials do in our name is not an acceptable choice. Responsible citizenship requires that we endeavor to become better informed on vital issues and active in the democratic processes we rightly cherish.

Our exploration in the first three chapters has underlined the nature of our relationships as well as our obligations as people of faith and citizens. But when events and issues look as complex as they do in the Middle East, even the best intentioned people can feel immobilized. As we face such issues in the 1990s, we naturally ask what, really, can we do? Short of becoming Middle East experts, in what ways can we make significant contributions to a larger process of reconciliation and peacemaking?

Concerned people can accomplish many constructive things, particularly in the areas of partnership in ministry, education and advocacy within our societies, and creative new efforts in inter-religious understanding and cooperation. Few people are able to be involved actively in all three arenas. But this should not inhibit doing what we can. Active involvement in even one of these realms is important, especially as that involvement touches the lives of others. Collectively, our varied efforts can make a great deal of difference. Where do we begin?

Commitment to partnership with the churches in the Middle East is basic. In practical terms, this means that North American and Middle Eastern Christians must endeavor to understand and take seriously one another's concerns, needs, priorities, hopes and fears.

To do so, we must know one another better. One way to begin is with education. Broadly based study programs are a start. For individuals and churches that wish to go deeper, many resources are available. Study that focuses on particular communions, the churches in a given country or specific ministries carried out through the Middle East Council of Churches is often rewarding. In many instances, denominational boards and agencies have done a great deal of work preparing resources. Before duplicating the efforts of others, it is wise to seek information within one's communion and in appropriate ecumenical agencies. Timely and helpful resources may exist already.

Education through Personal Encounter

Studying and learning about others takes on a new and deeper meaning when people meet face to face. One important form of encounter is visits by Middle Eastern Christians to North America. Opportunities abound. Individual churches, denominational judicatories, local and regional councils of churches as well as denominations and other national bodies can organize speaking tours, conferences and special programs featuring Middle Eastern Christians. Scores of knowledgeable, articulate and multilingual Middle Eastern Christians visit Canada and the U.S. each year. Inquiries through denominational or ecumenical channels will often reveal that appropriate people and programs are available.

The most frequent opportunities for personal encounter with Middle Eastern Christians happen when North Americans travel. Several hundred thousand Christians go each year on special tours to the Holy Land. A close look at current tour patterns and possible options will help those who want to nurture responsible partnership within the churches.

For most Holy Land tourists, the opportunity to learn first-hand about the Christian community living today in the birthplace of the church simply never arises. Far too often, organized tours feature tight itineraries that concentrate on historic sites. In the process, the vast majority of Western visitors never encounter the living church. In the rush to view and take pictures of stone monuments, many fail even to see what the apostle Peter called the "living stones" who form the church.

Not all Holy Land tours focus on places of antiquity. Many place the major emphasis on contemporary events in Israel. This is especially true of the "free" or highly subsidized tours provided by the government of Israel. Each year, several thousand U.S. and Canadian clergy accept invitations for inexpensive trips to the Holy Land. Not surprisingly, these tours feature considerable emphasis on particular Israeli views concerning the development of the land, the processes leading to statehood, central issues present at the time, conflicts, and so forth. While these are important elements, they do not provide for a very balanced understanding. Not only are Palestinian Arab views lacking, but the visitors often fail to experience the diversity within the Israeli Jewish community.

Holy Land Tourism   Many Christians also travel to the Middle East under the leadership of North Americans who emphasize the contemporary scene for other reasons. These Christians understand modern-day Israel as playing a central role in what they perceive as the unfolding drama of biblical prophecy. The theological frame of reference, often rooted in nineteenth-century premillennialism, interprets contemporary world events as vital components of the final stage of human history. The theological schemes vary, but most include the appearance of the anti-Christ, the second coming of Christ, and a massive conflagration at the battle of Armageddon. All the major events, according to this understanding, are centered in and around Israel.

Grace Halsell has written extensively about such religious/ political dynamics in her book *Prophecy and Politics*. Twice, in 1983 and 1985, Halsell joined tour groups led by the Rev. Jerry Falwell. The groups were large — each with over 600 participants. In her con-

versations with other pilgrims, Halsell discovered that their views on
the end times (derived from selective interpretation of various portions of the Bible) were woven together with seemingly uncritical
support for all Israeli policies. These views were reinforced by their
experiences and their highly political itinerary on the trips:

> On each Falwell tour, we listened to generals and politicians
> and visited Israeli farms, battlefields and shrines to the dead.
> ...On each tour, I attempted to count the hours we spent at
> Christian sites and hearing about Christ, and the time we spent
> learning the political and military accomplishments of the Zion-
> ist state. I came up with a ratio of one to 30. That is, for every
> hour for Christ's teachings, we spent about 30 hours on the
> political-military aspects of Israeli life.*

Middle Eastern Christians are often frustrated by Holy Land tourism. They see the masses of Western Christians come, have intense
experiences, and yet remain unaware of the vigorous debates within
the very society they are visiting. Many visitors return to North
America thinking that Israel is some kind of monolithic entity. Far
from it. Groups must have a very limited focus to miss the diversity present within the Israeli body politic, not to mention the Arab
community.

Middle Eastern Christians also observe how the well-organized
"religious right" has become an influential force in American politics — particularly in relation to the Middle East. How, they ask, can
hundreds of thousands of Christians make such an effort to come
to the lands of the Bible and yet seem so oblivious to the living
communities of faith in those lands?

Regrettably, many Westerners, particularly those with sharply defined theological and political agendas, appear to be uninterested in
the Middle Eastern Christians — and indeed, in any other Christians
who do not share their worldview. But many others who travel to
the Middle East are simply unaware. Once they discover the living
churches, they readily seek opportunities for interaction and fellowship. For many Western pilgrims, the problem is more an issue of
education than of ideology. The experience of the Portland-based
Mercy Corps International illustrates the point.

Mercy Corps is a Christian relief, development and educational
organization whose theological roots are in the evangelical tradi-

---

*Grace Halsell, *Prophecy and Politics: The Secret Alliance Between Israel and the
U.S. Christian Right*, rev. ed. (Chicago: Lawrence Hill Books, 1986), pp. 121–22.

tion. In addition to their humanitarian assistance programs around the world, they provide educational opportunities so that those who support their ministries can know more about the root causes and circumstances of the problems Mercy Corps seeks to address. In the Middle East, their work has included study tours for American evangelical leaders. Between 1986 and 1991, they have taken more than 20 groups to the region. In each instance, the church leaders, academics, journalists and others in these groups have returned home with a new awareness of the dynamics in the Middle East. They have discovered how much they need ways to rethink basic presuppositions and to understand the concerns, hopes and fears of all the people in the region.

Such educational trips enable participants to go beyond the barriers erected by one kind of propaganda or another and begin to wrestle with issues — theological, ideological and political — in new ways. It is heartening to see well-intentioned people, whatever their theological persuasion, discover and begin to take seriously the real-life consequences of their attitudes and behavior as these affect the lives of people in the Middle East.

The Importance of Planning   In the mid-1980s, the Middle East Council of Churches (MECC) established an Ecumenical Travel Office (ETO) to assist visitors and religious pilgrims. The ETO works with each group to help plan some or all of its itinerary. Their goal is to help each group realize its primary objectives as well as for travelers to broaden their experience through contact with a wide diversity of people and groups in the region. The ETO is especially geared to assist groups traveling in Israel/Palestine, Jordan, Syria, Egypt, Cyprus and Lebanon, so long as conditions allow for safe travel. Scores of Canadian, U.S., British, German, and Australian groups related to churches have discovered how rewarding it is to include meetings and worship experiences with Middle Eastern churches in their schedule.

People traveling with pre-arranged tour groups can also find ways to make connections with local Christians. They should seek out their tour leaders early and ask questions about the itinerary. Be sure a representative range of views will be heard during the visit. Christians can ask specifically for opportunities to meet with local Christians. Even if arrangements cannot be made in advance, it is often possible to make connections while traveling. If the schedule is full, consider an additional meeting or two during free time or in place of the modifications most tour groups experience routinely. If leaders are reluctant to help with such encounters, probe deeper to understand why. Are there unstated agendas? If so, what are they?

When planning a trip to the Middle East, it is wise to seek guidance. Denominational and/or ecumenical offices related to the Middle East should be able to help with planning and scheduling. The staff can also help link groups with the ETO. Having taken many groups throughout the Middle East, I know the value of such planning. Although no two groups have the same reasons for travel, it is certainly possible to spend a great deal of time visiting biblical and historical sites and still have time for meeting with various people. It is, after all not only the issues but also the lives and perspectives of people that weave together to make the colorful fabric of contemporary Middle Eastern life.

The most successful educational experiences are those that include a range of perspectives on religious and political issues. When in Jerusalem, for instance, include meetings with Israeli officials, peace activists and academic and religious leaders. Make time to visit the Knesset (Israel's Parliament) and Yad Vashem (the Holocaust museum and memorial). Learn how Israel is receiving and incorporating large numbers of Soviet and Ethiopian emigrés into their society. If possible, travel to a kibbutz (collective farm) and a settlement in the Occupied Territories. Some of these experiences require special planning. Many organizations, such as the Canadian Jewish Congress in Montreal or the American Jewish Committee in New York, are generally pleased to provide assistance or suggestions for church travel groups. Again, consultation with denominational offices is valuable.

Personal Connections   By all means, Western visitors should endeavor to experience the rich diversity of life and views within the Israeli Jewish community. But do not stop there. Be sure to include the contemporary Arab community as well, both Christian and Muslim. Seek out and learn about the experiences and perspectives of Israeli Arabs, the 700,000 Arabs with Israeli citizenship living within the 1967 borders of Israel. Christian shopkeepers and guides are easily found in traditional Christian tourist stops such as Nazareth in the Galilee region. Even casual encounters in normal interaction can be instructive.

More deliberate meetings and focused conversations are helpful in several ways. In the Galilee region, for instance, a visiting group can plan to meet with Father Elias Chacour, a Greek Catholic

(Melkite) priest in Ibillin, a traditional village located between Naza-reth and Haifa. The church, retreat center and high school show one aspect of Father Chacour's ministries. In one hour with Chacour, vis-itors will learn about a living church in the hills where Jesus walked with his disciples. Smiling children beam when they see him. Chris-tians and Muslims alike greet Chacour with the title, *abuna* ("our father"). Their demeanor reveals the love and respect they feel for him. The church is very much alive here. But all is not well. In conversation, Chacour will explain the problems facing Israeli Arabs, even as he makes clear his commitment to work for reconciliation.

There are many Christian leaders in Galilee who regularly meet with Western visitors to their homeland. Father Chacour is distinctive in that he has written eloquently about his life and ministry. His two books should be required reading for Christians planning to visit the Holy Land, or for anyone who simply wants to know more about the work of the church in the Middle East today.*

Seek out and learn from the perspectives of Palestinian Arabs living under military occupation in the West Bank and Gaza. Again, this is not difficult or dangerous but does require some planning. The visit can be incorporated into a trip to Bethlehem, for instance, a town adjacent to Jerusalem in the West Bank. Groups of Chris-tians regularly meet with Elias Freij, the mayor of Bethlehem, whose office overlooks Manger Square. There are many options — from universities, churches and mosques to refugee camps — for Western visitors who wish to understand the hopes, fears and concerns of Palestinians living under military occupation.

Many travel itineraries include visits to Jordan, Egypt, Cyprus or Syria. In each of these countries there are numerous ways to connect with the local churches. Again, planning is essential to make the most of the visit. When in Damascus, for instance, go to the "street called Straight" and see the place where Paul was let down in a basket. But also visit schools, churches and social service projects to see the people and churches engaged in ministry.

For hundreds of thousands of Western Christians, Holy Land tourism is the primary way of connecting personally with Christians in the Middle East. We should make the most of it. With thoughtful

---

*Elias Chacour and David Hazard, *Blood Brothers: A Palestinian Struggles for Reconciliation in the Middle East* (Tarrytown, N.Y.: Revell, Chosen Books, 1988); Elias Chacour and Mary E. Jensen, *We Belong to the Land: The Story of a Palestinian Israeli Who Lives for Peace and Reconciliation* (San Francisco: HarperCollins, 1990).

planning and preparation, these richly rewarding spiritual journeys can also strengthen the larger work of the church.

Mission and Service Ministries

The more we know about the history and present circumstances of Middle Eastern Christians, the more we know of the larger body of the church and our place within it. Western churches, blessed with material resources as well as structures for pursuing mission worldwide, must seek to shape programs not simply by what we think is needed but by what all can commonly affirm as priorities. Many churches, particularly those within the ecumenical family, are working to incorporate this approach to mutuality in mission. In the Middle East, this approach means recognizing:

> that the Middle East churches provide the essential witness to Christ in the Middle East.... The relationship presumes the equality of partners in every respect....
>
> The geographical considerations that informed past comity agreements among the western Protestant and Anglican churches, while a sign of western Christian cooperation in their time, are no longer appropriate since Middle East evangelical churches have developed their own autonomy and relationships. Future relationships should give evidence of unity and mutual respect among the churches.*

Middle Eastern Christians have much to share with the Christian community in the West. They are discovering new strength and vitality in cooperative, ecumenical mission and service programs. Middle Eastern Christians also have wisdom born of experience concerning Christian presence and witness in pluralistic societies. They have discovered the importance of knowing the beliefs and practices of their neighbors; they have learned when and how to bear witness through proclamation as well as through action. Learning from those who have lived for centuries with people of faith in other religious traditions is more important now than ever. The perspectives shared with us by Middle Eastern Christians can urge us to broaden our priorities for mission in North America. They can give us guidance in our ever-growing interaction with other people of faith.

---

*NCC "Middle East Policy Statement," p. 3.

The tower of the Lutheran Church of the Redeemer in Jerusalem, seen from the top of the Church of the Holy Sepulchre. (Photo: World Council of Churches)

Respectful Collaboration   At the same time, Western Christian churches have a great deal to share in partnership with churches in the Middle East. Traditional ministries in fields such as education, medical work and agricultural development remain essential. Denominational mission boards continue to provide personnel to fill critical positions in these and other specialized areas when churches in the Middle East cannot find the necessary people among the indigenous community. But the decisions need to be made through mutual consultation and planning. Such partnerships are producing new patterns of personnel placements. Some examples from the 1980s demonstrate the changing patterns.

Mark and Susanna Brown went to Jerusalem as missionaries appointed by the American Lutheran Church (subsequently the Evangelical Lutheran Church in America) in 1984 after four years of teaching and language study in Cairo and Amman. In addition to part-time teaching responsibilities and part-time pastoral duties within the Evangelical Lutheran Church of Jordan, Mark assisted the MECC when church-related study groups visited Israel and the Occupied Territories. Susanna assisted in this work while devoting most of her energy to their two small children.

By 1985, the need for the ecumenical ministry in Jerusalem had become especially important. Consequently, the MECC, the Lutherans and the National Council of Churches in the U.S.A. consulted about possible options. The result: The Browns were reassigned as full-time staff working for the MECC. The Lutherans seconded the Browns, that is, provided the financial support necessary for them to work full-time as MECC liaisons based in Jerusalem. For the next six years, Mark and Susanna became a critical link for dozens of groups visiting the Holy Land with the Palestinian Christian community and other Palestinians.

In 1985, the MECC communicated with various councils of churches in Europe and North America, requesting a physical therapist for rehabilitation work in Lebanon. Church World Service had provided two dozen physicians, nurses and therapists to Lebanon from 1982 to 1984 on both short- and long-term assignments. In this instance, the response came from the Canadian Council of Churches (CCC). After appropriate consultations, interviews and preparation, the CCC sent two people to Lebanon. In addition to the physical therapist, Sandra Ballentyne, the Presbyterian Church in Canada seconded Douglas du Charme to the MECC. His work, noted in chapter 2 above, included teaching part-time at the Near East School of Theology in Beirut and working part-time with the MECC's Emergency Relief, Rehabilitation and Reconstruction program in Lebanon. Working during a chaotic civil war, both Sandra and Douglas made enormous contributions over several years to the vital ministries provided through the MECC.

Benjamin and Carol Weir began their work as Presbyterian missionaries in Lebanon in 1953. For 31 years they worked in various ministries of the Presbyterian churches in the Synod of Syria and Lebanon. Their ministries changed as their church expanded its relationships with other churches there. When Ben was taken hostage in Beirut in 1984, both he and Carol were teaching at the Near East School of Theology and working in local churches. The compelling story of their ordeal during Ben's captivity is told in their book, *Hostage Bound, Hostage Free*. Woven into the book is a testimony to their love for the people of Lebanon — including the frustrated and angry Shi'ite Muslims who seized Ben. Their story reveals an inclusive, cooperative understanding of mutual mission at work.

In the late 1980s the United Methodist Church in the U.S. indicated a strong desire to become more directly involved in Middle Eastern ministries. This large communion had a history of mission work in North Africa — Tunisia and Algeria — but not in the eastern Mediterranean area. Resources, both personnel and financial, were available, but the precise nature the mission involvement should take was unclear. An interesting debate ensued. Some United Methodists wanted to establish a Methodist church in Jerusalem. But the Board of Global Missions, working with the MECC, identified a priority that centered not on a visible Methodist presence but on the best way to strengthen the existing Christian ministries in the Middle East. A new position was created, in Jerusalem. The missionary, Romeo del Rosario, was assigned to work part-time assisting the MECC liaison office and part-time with the Anglican Bishopric in Jerusalem. After three years, the arrangement appears to be a very good one.

These examples and various other cooperative mission efforts depend on the support local churches provide. Yet far too often, church members are not aware of the constructive and hopeful work they are helping to support. Educational programs during times of mission emphasis are one good way explore the new ways Christians worldwide are today working cooperatively in mutual mission.

Service Ministries   Perhaps the most visible and far-reaching way North Americans are working with Middle Eastern Christians is through their support for human service ministries. In chapter 2 we discussed some aspects of these vital ministries in relation to the Gulf war, the conflict in Lebanon and the longstanding work with Palestinian refugees.

Another major program is carried out through the Bishopric for Public, Ecumenical and Social Services in Egypt's Coptic Orthodox Church. Each year, churches from Europe and North America provide substantial resources (approximately $1 million per year from 1986 to 1991) to assist in programs that reach into every diocese in Egypt. In the midst of dismal economic conditions, the bishopric supports numerous critical social service projects — from prenatal clinics and preschool programs to vocational training in carpentry and garbage reclamation projects. The projects will not end the spiral of poverty in Egypt. They do offer hope and opportunity for many who would otherwise have none.

North American churches — individually and through the Canadian and National Councils of Churches — provide financial, material aid and, occasionally, personnel support for the Coptic Orthodox Church program as well as the various MECC programs described earlier. These resources come through various channels in different churches. Make an effort to learn more about the ways your church is involved through ecumenical channels or directly in support of this and other diaconal ministries of Middle Eastern churches.*

The largest U.S. source of ecumenical funding for emergency humanitarian and social service ministries comes through Church World Service and Witness (CWSW). Local communities all across the land organize CROP walks each year. Many of the participants are active in churches working ecumenically; many are not. In Charlotte, North Carolina, for instance, the scene of the largest annual CROP walk, more than half of the 6,000 participants are Southern Baptists. In some communities, Jewish participation is substantial. Through CROP walks people who are not affiliated with churches directly involved with cooperative ecumenical ministries can and do contribute a great deal.

Various international human service programs work closely with the MECC and Middle Eastern churches. Organizations such as Save the Children and the Christian Children's Fund are both ecumenical in orientation and cooperative in their style of ministry. Such organizations provide another way for concerned people to help others help themselves. Before supporting a particular group, it is wise to learn as much as possible about its style of work, how its resources are allocated, and so forth.

Participating in a CROP walk or other effort for funding humanitarian services will not bring peace to the Middle East. It will contribute meaningfully to a wide range of domestic and international programs that are meeting emergency needs as well as providing skills for self-sufficiency. In many cases, such as in Lebanon, the Gulf war and among Palestinians, these efforts are related directly to the larger processes of peacemaking and reconciliation. Whatever

---

*Some denominations participate through annual offerings such as One Great Hour of Sharing. In many denominations, their service agencies — the United Methodist Committee on Relief, the Presbyterian Hunger Fund, the Week of Compassion Fund of the Christian Church (Disciples of Christ), Lutheran World Relief, the Presiding Bishops Fund for World Relief, and the like — also contribute directly to various ecumenical ministries.

the route you take, learn more about and get involved with these tangible ways to assist people in need. In the process, you are doing some of the things that make for peace.

Facing the Future

Although such ministries are heartening and meet many needs, there are causes for deep concern. For many Christians in the historic lands of the Bible, the future is very uncertain. In several areas the unsettled political dynamics creates pressures, particularly on minority communities. In conflicts where religious understanding shapes political behavior, such as in Lebanon and Iran, communities may be isolated, feel disenfranchised or experience overt discrimination. Frequently, minority communities find economic opportunities more limited than they are for the majority.

Many Middle Eastern Christians have emigrated to the West over the past century; many others may soon follow unless there is real movement toward resolution of daunting political problems in their lands. Pastors and church officials in Jerusalem, for instance, report precipitous declines in their communities in recent decades. They tell us that current trends may result in the eventual disappearance of Christians in the Holy Land.

In short, the physical and material needs of Middle Eastern people living in difficult circumstances or caught in debilitating strife are real and urgent. Even more important, however, is the need for equitable political solutions. Christians in the Middle East appeal for help to end the ongoing human suffering and, at the same time, help that will enable them to remain as a vital presence in their homelands. They urge Christians and others of goodwill in the West to focus their energies on Middle East education and public policy advocacy.

RELIEF IN IRAQ

Reports from an MECC ERRR visit to Iraq in July 1991 by Miss Suad Hajj and Mr. Mike Nahhal from ERRR Lebanon.

The South. The visits paid to the towns of Kout, Amara, Qurneh and Basra revealed extensive destruction which is the consequence of the Iraq-Iran war, the Gulf war and the recent civil uprising. Most of the bridges, plants, and major infrastructures were bombarded or burnt.

The Basra district now counts 1.5 million people who stayed on, in spite of the war which raged around them. A large majority of the population fled to Baghdad and the north during the last events. The beautiful port of Basra and the Shatt al Arab river, where Sindbad sailed from, are now still and surrounded by burnt private properties, shops and houses.

In southern Iraq for many years dates constituted the principal agricultural export. The palm tree has proliferated in the south because of saturated soil and extremely hot climate. The hot and humid wind of the south still blows but large surfaces of palm forests are burnt due to shelling or cut down by people for use as cooking fire.

Contacts were made with UNICEF, ICRC and the Governorate of Health. Visits were also paid to hospitals and clinics in order to study the needs and possible ways of distributing relief material sent through ERS including the milk shipment donated by the Mennonites Central Committee.

We also visited the churches of Basra and discussed needs and future relief distribution. The Evangelical, Armenian Catholic, Latin and Syrian Orthodox faithful come to worship at the Syrian Catholic or Chaldean churches in Basra because some priests have left the area. People share with one another their daily burdens.

The presence of NGO's is not very obvious. However, ICRC, UNICEF, and Médecins Sans Frontières are working in the area. Save the Children Federation seconded its staff to work jointly with UNICEF. Most of the NGO humanitarian aid was concentrated on water and sanitation. Food relief distribution was minimal.

The North. The north of Iraq is a mountainous region which consists of several parallel ranges, separated by long deep valleys drained by rivers that flow into the Tigris. In this region, a lot of villages lying on the boarder between Iraq, Turkey and Iran are destroyed and large settlements are established in those valleys....

Our visit to the northern region included Kirkuk, Sulaymanieh, Arbil and Mosul. We were very efficiently assisted there by the personnel sent by Danchurchaid [Denmark] to support MECC work in relief, rehabilitation and reconstruction. These included persons working in the fields of health, electricity, plumbing and logistics. In these areas, families were seen brought back to their villages or settlements from across the borders in U.N. trucks. One could also see at check-points the Pesh Mergas, the Kurdish armed militias, sitting together with the Iraqi soldiers.

In Sulaymanieh, we attended Mass at the Chaldean church, which was remarkably crowded. Some Christian Kurds were also present. We met with Bishop Abdul Ahad and some Christian families. Some of them who used to afford a holiday in Lebanon are now waiting for any assistance to help them meet their daily needs. In the same district, a visit was paid to Sayyid Sadek, a Kurdish village which is now under the control of the Pesh Mergas. Like many others, this village is destroyed and the inhabitants live in tents next to their agricultural fields.

We also visited the district of Mosul. Christians there are dispersed in twelve villages and count around 8,000 families. In that region, we had the opportunity to meet Bishop Luka at his famous Monastery of Mar Matta, built in 381 A.D. and located at 40 kilometres from the city of Mosul. In the city, the Iraqi Red Crescent appointed a physician to accompany us throughout our visits to the various hospitals and medico-social centres. Our visit to the churches was concluded with a meeting at the Syrian Orthodox Bishopric. The Christians of Mosul city constitute a minority group. They are Chaldeans (2,500 families), Syrian Orthodox (1,500 families), Syrian Catholic (1,000 families), Assyrians (300 families), Armenians (160 families) and Latins (40 families).

Home Visits. At the request of the local churches, we made field visits with the help of the local priests in order to understand living conditions, as well as define needs and priorities. Each visit carried out to needy families in various areas and communities always revealed endemic poverty, a wish for emigration, deep grief caused by 11 years of continuous war, and loss of relatives.

The report continues to describe meetings with staff of other humanitarian agencies and food, health and redevelopment needs as well as aid already received from church relief agencies around the world, from Europe to the United States and Canada to Taiwan and elsewhere. From WCC Report, August 10, 1991.

EDUCATION FOR RESPONSIBLE CITIZENSHIP

Responsible citizenship begins with education. We must work at this consciously since we approach the Middle East with a good deal of intellectual and emotional baggage. We have much to learn and, at points, things to unlearn. The issues are many, but we can go a long way in understanding them.

Study tours to the Middle East and programs featuring Middle Eastern Christians, Muslims and Jews here in North America not only enhance ecumenical relations, they also offer opportunity for education in political issues. Visiting groups should seek meetings with their own nation's foreign service personnel, for instance, while in Tel Aviv, Cairo or Amman. Ask them about operative government policies. Seek to understand what is being done in your name and why from officials who represent your government. Further, trips to the Middle East can help us start thinking about what kinds of political action would be most constructive. Ask various Israelis, Palestinians, Egyptians, Syrians and others what specific policies and actions they believe the Western powers should take.

Obviously, one need not travel to the Middle East to seek out the views of Jews, Christians, Muslims or others who are related directly to the Middle East. Study programs and lecture series in churches or through universities and seminaries offer ways to learn from a variety of people. Sometimes it is possible to organize a dialogue with two or more people whose views differ. Study programs might include films or videotapes. Several documentaries and feature programs produced each year examine Middle East issues. Be alert for programs prepared by the Canadian Broadcasting Corporation, Canada's National Film Board and Public Broadcasting Stations in the U.S. Such resources can usefully supplement our learning.

Frequently, there are valuable human resources right in our midst. Thousands of Middle Eastern students enroll in Canadian and U.S. universities each year. These students, like the scores of Egyptians, Syrians, Iranians, Israelis and others who now live in North America, are very closely connected with families and friends in their native lands. Many welcome inquiries about their views, their concerns, their frustrations. Getting to know our Middle Eastern neighbors — Jewish, Christian and Muslim — who live in our midst can be one of the most helpful ways to educate ourselves and others in our churches.

A number of denominational bodies have produced resources specifically for churches. Inquire about study packets, videos and other resources produced or recommended by staff persons with responsibilities for the Middle East or education within the churches.

Policy Statements

Some communions have prepared and adopted policy statements and/or detailed resolutions dealing with the Middle East. Most such documents reflect the concerted efforts of a group or committee commissioned to report after extensive study and consultation. The United Methodist Church, for example, adopted a major resolution on the Israeli/Palestinian conflict at its last General Conference in 1988. The Presbyterian Church (U.S.A.) has prepared and adopted substantial resolutions at General Assembly meetings each year for the past decade. Other U.S. denominations have chosen to adopt formally the NCC Policy Statement on the Middle East as their own. These and other policy statements and resolutions continue to have great value as educational tools. When they are read and studied, they can help raise the level of informed debate within the churches by helping concerned Christians focus on key issues for thoughtful, prayerful action.

In 1989, the Canadian Council of Churches (CCC) adopted a policy document to guide its member churches in their relations and work with Middle Eastern churches. The section dealing with public policy advocacy reflects how Canadian churches and their government relate more cooperatively than is the case for many churches in the U.S.:

Over the years the Canadian government has attempted to be constructive and even-handed in its policy toward the conflicts in the Middle East. Although Canadian actions have not always been as even-handed as the policy would indicate, there is a perception in the region that Canada is fair-minded and sincerely concerned to promote peace. Canadians can take pride in, for example, the work of Canadian troops in peace-keeping forces over the years in Cyprus, the Sinai, Lebanon, the Golan Heights and Jerusalem. We recognize with appreciation the humanitarian aid provided by the Canadian International Development Assistance (CIDA) for the relief of suffering in the region. We urge the Canadian government to use its position in the region in support of diplomatic initiatives for peace negotiations.*

The CCC and several of its member churches have become increasingly active on Middle East education, mutual mission and public policy advocacy during the past decade. In 1986, the CCC formed a Middle East Working Group; in 1987, the CCC sponsored an official delegation visit to the Middle East; and, since 1989, several MECC staff, including Gabriel Habib, the general secretary, have visited churches in Canada in response to invitations.

One of the most far-reaching major church studies in North America has come from the U.S. Conference of Catholic Bishops. In November 1989, the bishops adopted a lengthy pastoral letter entitled, "Toward Peace in the Middle East: Perspectives, Principles and Hopes." The bishops identified their role (and, by extension, the role of other concerned Christians in North America) and angle of vision early in the text:

> We write this statement first and foremost as pastors and religious leaders concerned about what continuing conflict and violence mean for the people who live there, for all the world and for people of faith everywhere. Our religious convictions, our traditional teaching and our ecclesial responsibilities call us to stand with the suffering, to advocate dialogue in place of violence and to work for genuine justice and peace.
>
> ...We have sought in these reflections to state our concerns clearly, with balance and restraint and with genuine respect and appreciation for the strong feelings and deep convictions of others....People of good will can sometimes disagree without undermining fundamental relationships of respect. We hope our reflections will be perceived in this context.†

The document discusses two specific arenas of conflict: Lebanon and the Israeli/Palestinian conflict. Recognizing other major issues, the pastoral letter zeroed in on these two because of their urgency, their importance for Christians in the region and the challenges they pose for U.S. policy.

---

*The full text of the 1989 position paper of the Canadian Council of Churches is available through the CCC, 40 St. Clair Avenue East, Toronto, Ontario M4T 1M9.

†"Toward Peace in the Middle East: Perspectives, Principles and Hopes," by the U.S. Catholic Bishops, p. 1. Copies of the statement are $2.95 plus $1.50 postage from USCC Publishing, 3211 Fourth St., N.E., Washington, DC 20017.

It is often hard to measure the effects of church pronouncements and resolutions on public policies. The churches understand well the limits of such statements. At the same time, Christians must take seriously their responsibility as people of faith and as citizens. Depending on the breadth of distribution and seriousness of the debate public statements engender, the potential significance is considerable. Quite apart from any measurable "success," the bishops' pastoral letter and the resolutions and policy statements of other churches accomplish several goals.

First, they make clear the Christian responsibility to engage faithfully in ministry that is pastoral, prophetic and reconciling. Second, they underscore our interconnectedness and the interdependence of the world community in ways that evoke empathetic concern for people caught in unjust or tragic circumstances. One result of this heightened concern should be a desire to participate in constructive change.

Third, the pastoral letter and policy statements, unlike virtually all media coverage of Middle East events, demonstrate that it is possible to understand and identify basic issues as well as appropriate steps to address the issues. These documents provide clarity without being simplistic and hope without being unrealistic. Those who read and ponder such carefully prepared texts will not easily retreat into noninvolvement because "the issues are too complex."

The pastoral letter prepared by the U.S. Conference of Bishops offers a perspective that many Protestants and Orthodox Christians do not regularly see in ecumenical structures. Used as part of a study process, this document can help us reach across communion lines and make new connections within the church. This broadening ecumenism is especially significant since, in 1990, the various Catholic communions formally became full members of the Middle East Council of Churches. While North American communions are not presently at such a stage of ecumenical closeness, we do need to learn from one another as together we approach issues of paramount importance to the Orthodox, Catholic and Protestant Christians living in the lands where the church began.

Public Policy Advocacy

Education is not, of course, an end in itself; it should lead toward action. The kind of action most Middle Eastern Christians consistently encourage falls in the realm of public policy advocacy. We take this action in our role as citizens — specifically acting from concerns as Christians.

Several major denominations and denominational groups have developed Middle East advocacy networks. Among the most active is the Presbyterian Advocates on the Middle East. The Washington Office of the Presbyterian Church (U.S.A.) mails packets to the "advocates," including specific information about pending legislation, analysis of key policy decisions as well as reprints of important articles. Suggestions for particular action — phone calls, letters, fax messages to members of Congress and the Administration — are also included, usually when key issues on which the church has a policy position arise.

Another strong education and advocacy network is the Quaker-based American Friends Service Committee (AFSC). Its Middle East peace education network is coordinated through the headquarters in Philadelphia and regional offices around the country. The AFSC publishes materials and establishes action priorities in consultation with its Washington office, the Middle East program staff and the committee working in the region. The collective wisdom from the AFSC's longstanding Middle East work has created a superb study, *A Compassionate Peace: A Future for Israel, Palestine, and the Middle East.*

In the wake of the 1991 Gulf war, a new church-related network was born within the Reformed Church in America (RCA), a denomination with more than a century of mission history in the Gulf region. In its first few months, however, Middle East Peace Makers grew beyond the RCA to embrace a wide ecumenical constituency. Many prominent church leaders (Protestant, Catholic and Orthodox) and several major denominations (including the American Baptist Churches, Armenian Orthodox Church, Church of the Brethren, Evangelical Lutheran Church in America and the Friends United Meeting) endorsed the effort in 1991.

Middle East Peace Makers provides North American Christians with a network for mutual support and regular access to current information and resources. To pursue peacemaking — within the church, with people of other faiths and among the nations — the network publishes a monthly newsletter of useful resources. Middle East Peace Makers promises to be a good channel for constructive involvement, particularly for people in churches that do not have their own education and advocacy networks.

In the U.S., these various efforts converge and connect in Washington D.C., with Churches for Middle East Peace (C-MEP). Started in 1984 when a number of churches sought ways to enhance their Middle East public policy advocacy work, C-MEP has grown to include some 20 communions and church-related organizations with offices in Washington. In less than a decade, C-MEP has become a well-respected organization on Capitol Hill.

In view of the diversity of Middle East issues, C-MEP concentrates its energies in the areas of peace processes, human rights, arms sales and transfers, terrorism, and the status of Jerusalem. Working cooperatively, C-MEP members monitor developments, track legislation, meet with people in government and facilitate meetings between visiting church representatives and government officials.

The most direct way for individuals to support C-MEP is through active participation in one of the education and advocacy networks discussed above. On several occasions, C-MEP has organized "advocacy days" in Washington, which invite active participation. Ask whether your communion is involved in C-MEP; and if not, encourage leaders to consider supporting this ecumenical effort both programmatically and financially.

Churches for Middle East Peace is one among many Middle East advocacy groups active in Washington. Some organizations, such as the America Israel Public Affairs Committee (AIPAC), are large, well-financed and powerful. Many groups, such as the American Arab Anti-Discrimination Committee (ADC), concentrate on particular issues connected to the Middle East. Many others concentrate on particular issues related to business interests such as oil, trade relations and arms exports.

By comparison, C-MEP and the related networks discussed above represent a modest effort, yet one that has begun to bear fruit. C-MEP, for example, now provides information and analysis for members of Congress, assists church representatives who offer testimony before Congress, and meets regularly with officials in the Department of State to clarify and discuss policy positions.

Education and advocacy are critical parts of a long-term agenda to enhance mutuality in mission and work toward peace, justice and reconciliation in society. The kinds of initiatives and programs we have outlined in this study require sustained efforts over a period of years. Building relations among churches, working cooperatively in ministry, pursuing educational programs and responsible public policy advocacy — this is a bold agenda that will carry the churches well into the twenty-first century.

Christians, of course, do not and will not speak with one voice on highly charged religious and political issues. There is room for considerable disagreement among people of faith and goodwill. In addition, specific issues and priorities will change and new ones will appear. Nevertheless, the call to responsible citizenship remains strong and clear. We must seek to be well-informed on issues and engaged constructively in the policy debates and decisions within our societies.

RESPONSIBLE INTERFAITH RELATIONS

Various issues and responsibilities are compelling for North American Christians. But we cannot isolate our views and actions as Christians. We began by stressing the Middle East as the religious heritage of all the children of Abraham. We return to that theme to place Christian concerns and actions into this wider perspective.

The lands of the Middle East mirror the pluralism and diversity in the larger world. The problems facing people there are not unlike those facing people in other nations. People who wish to contribute toward resolving these problems can and should look within their own religious tradition for wisdom and guidance. But at the same time they must recognize the perspectives, aspirations and contributions of others who share the concerns, but do not share the religious tradition.

The first goal in interfaith relations is understanding. Christians, Muslims and Jews have had a long and, at times, difficult history. Misunderstanding and antipathy have too often characterized their relations. It is now more important than ever for these descendants of Abraham to overcome the negative side of this history and work toward a more promising future.

This requires from Christians an intentional effort to learn more about Islam and Judaism as well as about the concerns, hopes and fears of their adherents. Better understanding is a critical step toward cooperation on issues of shared concern. Nowhere are the issues more urgent than in the Middle East. At the same time, the converging concerns of Jews, Christians and Muslims make this one of the most difficult areas for interreligious cooperation. This is especially the case with Jewish-Christian relations, where several factors are involved.

Jewish-Christian Relations

Most Jews feel a deep attachment to the state of Israel. They know that Israel has many problems, yet they are often slow to voice public criticism of Israeli policies. Many Jews in the West fear that public criticism may weaken support for Israel or strengthen its adversaries. Jews also know well the long history of Western Christian anti-Semitism, which, inexcusably, continues to this day. It is not surprising then that many Jews are suspicious of Christians who work

on Middle East issues. Acknowledging good intentions, while at the
same time expressing these fears, a rabbi once put it to me this way:
"It is not that we don't trust the Christians, but we are wary. Two
thousand years of 'Christian love' is almost more than we Jews can
bear!"

The rabbi's comment reflects a reality that Christians must bear in
mind. The dismal history of Western Christian attitudes and behavior toward Jews cannot be dismissed easily. It permeates communal
relations, most notably when controversial issues concerning Israel
are the focus of attention. Christian-Jewish efforts on Middle East
issues present both great obstacles and great opportunities. Finding constructive ways for Jews and Christians in North America to
understand and work together can contribute toward constructive
Middle East policy positions by our governments. It can also help
build a foundation for more hopeful future relations and cooperation
on a range of shared concerns within our societies.

Significant efforts in Christian-Jewish relations have been under
way for some years. More focused attention on Islam is only now
beginning to occur. Given the increasingly important role of Islam
on the world stage, the need to understand it more accurately is
urgent. The Gulf crisis and war raised the level of this awareness, or
the need for it, for many people in North America.

Ecumenical Programs

Many communions have specialized offices and programs that deal
directly with interfaith relations. Most Roman Catholic dioceses, for
instance, have someone responsible for this work. Check to see what
your church is doing or is planning to do. Many communions have
prepared valuable resources. Officials in your communion or others
who have been active at the local level can describe opportunities
for direct involvement — ranging from large international gatherings
to structured meetings in a local setting.

The United Methodist Church, for instance, has a long history of
interreligious efforts. In 1992, the church is scheduled to consider a
major resolution on Christian-Muslim relations at its General Conference. The process of preparing, debating and refining the document
will be instructive both for the Methodists and others who observe
the process as will the resulting resolution.

Some regional church organizations and individual congregations
are engaged in ongoing dialogue programs with Jews and Muslims.

While structured dialogue requires careful planning, it can be extraordinarily rewarding. An example from Greenville, South Carolina, illustrates the point.

In 1991, a local Presbyterian congregation decided to develop a three-month adult education series on Christian-Jewish and Christian-Muslim relations. They wanted to concentrate in particular on the way these relations connect with Middle East issues. They set up a program, including study materials, presentations and discussions. They invited Jewish and Muslim representatives to meet with them to be part of the process. The study worked well. Not only did the congregation grow in understanding as they had hoped, they discovered their Jewish and Muslim neighbors in a new way. They ended up being invited to visit the local mosque and a synagogue and thereby widen the connections. Other opportunities also began to surface, quite apart from the initial Middle East focus. Members of the church and the mosque began meeting to explore ways of working together on local issues, such as crime, drugs, and public education. Church members are hopeful that similar opportunities will develop with their Jewish neighbors.

Issues of interfaith understanding and cooperation are particularly well suited to ecumenical groups because the encounter is not primarily between Baptists and Muslims or Jews and Lutherans. Rather, the concerns are between Christians (collectively) and Muslims and Jews. Accordingly, ecumenical organizations have designed some helpful resources and programs to foster interfaith understanding and cooperation. Many local and regional councils of churches are actively involved. Some are religious councils that include Jewish and Muslim congregations in their membership. Look for these programs and opportunities in your local setting.

New Relationships

The Canadian Council of Churches and the National Council of Churches have worked extensively in interfaith relations for more than a decade. Both councils have staff who work full-time on a range of issues in the contemporary encounters between religious communities. On a global scale, the World Council of Churches and the Vatican have major interfaith programs. The WCC's subunit on Dialogue with People of Living Faiths and the Vatican's Pontifical Council on Interreligious Dialogue both produce thoughtful and stimulating resources to help Christians with interfaith issues. Middle East concerns, while not the primary focus of these ecumenical programs, are never far away when Christians, Muslims and Jews talk together.

One particular U.S.-based organization works explicitly at the crossroads of interfaith relations and Middle East issues. The U.S. Interreligious Committee for Peace in the Middle East was established in 1986 to bring together Jews, Christians and Muslims who agreed on the necessity for a negotiated settlement to the longstanding Israeli/Palestinian conflict. Among the more than 1,500 prominent religious leaders active in this organization are significant differences of opinion about the causes of conflict and the most productive steps toward peace. Many participants have been heartened to discover how much agreement exists on such key issues as self-determination, independence and security for both the Israelis and Palestinians.

This interreligious education and advocacy work is a sign of hope. It demonstrates that Jews, Christians and Muslims can find points of agreement and work together on even the most divisive issues, such as the path toward a just, secure and lasting peace in the Middle East. It also challenges the prevailing stereotypes about religious communities. They are not monolithic entities. Rather, they are made up of people of faith and goodwill. When people make the effort to meet one another as human beings, the stereotypes about the "other" are often dissipated and the possibilities for new, more positive relations begin to grow.

Work in interfaith relations is a long-term agenda. After centuries of mistrust and open hostility, there is a long road ahead. But we must travel that road together if we hope to help fashion a better future. The particular concerns that draw various communities to the Middle East provide a context for pursuing this agenda with our Jewish and Muslim neighbors.

THE CALL TO FAITHFULNESS

Throughout this book we have stressed repeatedly that there are no easy answers or simple solutions for Christians relating to people and events in the Middle East. We have outlined an agenda that calls for long-term efforts in several areas. Reasonable people might well ask how realistic are the chances for the success of these efforts to nurture relations among the churches, to educate ourselves, to be advocates in public policy or to encounter our neighbors of other faiths. The voice of experience says that a straightforward prediction for success or failure within a particular period would be neither possible nor wise. But this much is clear: As people of faith we are not called to be successful; we are called to be faithful. The ministry of Father Elias Chacour, the Greek Catholic priest in the Galilee, embodies this call to faithfulness.

Chacour's ministry in Ibillin includes social services and education in the church's schools that benefit Palestinian Christians and Muslims in the village. In the larger context of Israel, his ministry of reconciliation embraces all the children of Abraham. His efforts, like those of many others, call for nonviolent means to resolve the conflicts between Arabs and Jews in his homeland. Chacour's vision for the future is simple yet compelling:

> We need to create a new reality in Galilee, changing the situation from injustice and inequality between Palestinians and Jews to a true partnership of equals.... It is a matter of building bridges among members of the same family. Always there is the temptation of violence and might, but the ones who build bridges acknowledge, "My friend is also right, and I am also wrong...." This land, this Palestine, this Israel, does not belong to either Jews or Palestinians. Rather, we are compatriots who belong to the land and to each other. If we cannot live together, we surely will be buried here together. We must choose life.*

Father Chacour's effort to live out this vision is costly. At times, his message of reconciliation involves physical risk. After being attacked by an angry and frustrated villager wielding a knife, a

---

*Elias Chacour and Mary E. Jensen, *We Belong to the Land: The Story of a Palestinian Israeli Who Lives for Peace and Reconciliation* (San Francisco: HarperCollins, 1990), pp. 204–5.

man who had himself suffered greatly, Chacour reflected on his vulnerability and on his calling as a follower of Christ:

> How fragile and insignificant I really am, I thought. How easily I could lose my life, like paper in the wind, and it could happen in such a quick, senseless way. God knows I am ready to die, but I love to live, I love this beautiful earth and God's people, and I want to be a part of it as long as possible. I want to accomplish the tasks God has given me to do.... Am I not one of "God's deputies" on earth? The answer to hatred and violence is a genuine, personal initiative completely independent from the reaction to violence. Respecting human rights and protecting human life should never be a reaction to violence but should arise out of one's love for human beings, for life.... This is the message of the Man from Galilee.*

Christians in North America are privileged to work in mutual ministry with Father Chacour, the Coptic Orthodox Church in Egypt, the MECC and various other manifestations of the churches in the Middle East. We can support these ministries through prayer and by sharing resources. We are able also to bolster ministries of reconciliation in Israel/Palestine, Lebanon, Cyprus or wherever conflict exists. We can help make audible the voices for peace and justice even as we explore opportunities for improving education, interfaith relations, and public policy advocacy in our own settings.

Christians can be engaged directly in ministry related to the Middle East in many ways. As people of faith and hope, we must never underestimate precisely what God can do through our individual and collective efforts, no matter how modest they may appear. We may never even see the fruits of our efforts. But the call is not to be successful. We are called to be faithful. The people of the Middle East deserve our best efforts.

---

*We Belong to the Land, pp. 120–22.

Annotated Bibliography

Bergen, Kathy, David Neuhaus, and Ghassan Rubeiz, eds. *Justice and the Intifada: Palestinians and Israelis Speak Out*. New York: Friendship Press, 1991. A fascinating collection of interviews with Israeli and Palestinian activists, academics, women and religious leaders. Their varied insights and perspectives challenge readers to broaden their understanding of both the Palestinian "uprising" and the search for justice.

Birkland, Carol J. *Unified in Hope: Arabs and Jews Talk about Peace*. New York: Friendship Press, 1987. A helpful and hopeful collection of interviews with nineteen Israelis and Palestinians who are committed to a peaceful resolution of their longstanding conflict.

Chacour, Elias, and David Hazard. *Blood Brothers: A Palestinian Struggles for Reconciliation in the Middle East*. Tarrytown, N.Y.: Revell, Chosen Books, 1988.

Chacour, Elias, and Mary E. Jensen. *We Belong to the Land: The Story of a Palestinian Israeli Who Lives for Peace and Reconciliation*. San Francisco: HarperCollins, 1990. Father Chacour describes his calling as a peacemaker in his own land. See pages 97, 117.

Fenton, Thomas, and Mary Heffron, eds. *Middle East: A Directory of Resources*. Maryknoll, N.Y.: Orbis Books, 1988. A very helpful, though slightly dated directory of organizations, books, periodicals, pamphlets, articles and audiovisuals dealing with the contemporary Middle East. The entries are annotated.

Friedman, Thomas. *From Beirut to Jerusalem*. New York: Farrar, Straus, Giroux, 1989. A compelling assessment of the political dynamics in Lebanon, Syria and Israel during the 1980s. Friedman is a two-time Pulitzer Prize winner who spent a decade in Beirut and Jerusalem as bureau chief for the New York Times.

Fromkin, David. *A Peace to End All Peace: The Fall of the Ottoman Empire and the Creation of the Modern Middle East*. New York: Avon Books, 1989. A detailed account of the multisided external and internal political developments that shaped the Middle East in the first three decades of this century.

Halsell, Grace. *Prophecy and Politics: The Secret Alliance Between Israel and the U.S. Christian Right*. Rev. ed. Chicago: Lawrence Hill Books, 1986. A provocative account of the religious and political worldviews and

current activities of many North American Christians working closely
with Israel.

Horner, Norman A. *A Guide to the Christian Churches in the Middle East.*
Elkhart, Ind.: Mission Focus Publications, 1989. This book offers an
overview of the origins and present-day distribution of churches in the
Middle East as well as brief reflections on some issues facing churches
in the various countries.

Hourani, Albert. *A History of the Arab Peoples.* (Cambridge, Mass.: Harvard
University Press, 1991. A scholarly, but readable history of the Arabs
from the rise of Islam to the present day. This text by a major scholar
may well become a classic.

Kimball, Charles A. *Striving Together: A Way Forward in Christian-Muslim
Relations.* Maryknoll, N.Y.: Orbis Books, 1991. This text introduces the
interested nonspecialist to Islam and the challenging problems plaguing
Christian-Muslim relations. Practical and theological issues are explored
in an effort to discern and articulate a way forward for the adherents
in the world's two largest religious communities.

Mendelsohn, Everett. *A Compassionate Peace: A Future for Israel, Palestine,
and the Middle East.* Rev. ed. New York: Hill and Wang, 1989. A
thoughtful and accessible introduction to the major issues operative in
the Middle East. Prepared under the auspices of the American Friends
Service Committee, this book combines clear analysis with realistic
alternatives that can lead to a more just and peaceful future.

Rudin, A. James. *Israel for Christians: Understanding Modern Israel.* Philadelphia: Fortress Press, 1983. A helpful guide explaining the importance of
Israel, modern Zionism, Jerusalem and other key issues from a Jewish
perspective. As the title suggests, Rabbi Rudin addresses North American Christians, a community he knows well in his capacity as director
of Interreligious Affairs for the American Jewish Committee.

Speight, R. Marston. *God Is One: The Way of Islam.* New York: Friendship Press, 1989. A solid, popular introduction to Islam written for the
Christian community in North America.

Weir, Benjamin, and Carol Weir. *Hostage Bound, Hostage Free.* Louisville,
Ky.: Westminster/John Knox Press, 1987. Moving account of Ben Weir's
sixteen-month captivity in Lebanon and of Carol Weir's efforts to enlist
help for the hostages and understanding for the middle East.

Yergin, Daniel. *The Prize: The Epic Quest for Oil, Money and Power.* New
York: Simon & Schuster, 1991. A weighty, powerful and unsettling
narrative history of oil, the twentieth century's most prized commodity.